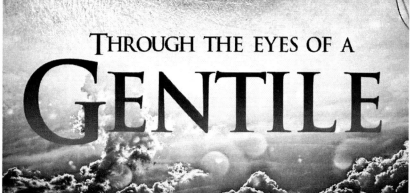

Through the Eyes of a Gentile
Copyright © 2015 Irene Laster
All rights reserved.

No part of this book may be reproduced in any form or by any electronic or mechanical means including information storage and retrieval systems, without permission in writing from the author. The only exception is by a reviewer, who may quote short excerpts in a review.

Publisher Contact:
irlaster@tampabay.rr.com

Scriptures taken from the Holy Bible, New International Version®, NIV®. Copyright © 1973, 1978, 1984, 2011 by Biblica, Inc.™ Used by permission of Zondervan. All rights reserved worldwide. www.zondervan.com The "NIV" and "New International Version" are trademarks registered in the United States Patent and Trademark Office by Biblica, Inc.™

NOTE: With permission of the NIV® publisher, all personal pronouns related to the Godhead have the first letter capitalized. In addition, Messianic Terminology has been used in place of the published NIV® text.

ISBN: 978-1-940164-38-0

Cover Design by Victor Daniel Diaz
Interior Design by Amy Cole, JPL Design Solutions

Printed in the United States of America

Contents

Introduction 5

Chapter 1: Broken Roads That Led Me to Yeshua 7

Chapter 2: Life as a Single Parent 15

Chapter 3: Deceived 23

Chapter 4: Money—The Answer 25

Chapter 5: My Family on Drugs 29

Chapter 6: Back to Square One 33

Chapter 7: A New Birth 35

Chapter 8: Making the Temple Ready for God 39

Chapter 9: God My Deliverer 43

Chapter 10: Expecting Quick Miracles 47

Chapter 11: Mama Luke 53

Chapter 12: Sin Deserving Death 61

Chapter 13: God My Healer 65

Chapter 14: Marriage in a Worldly Way 81

Chapter 15: God My Provider 91

Chapter 16: Growing to Maturity 99

Chapter 17: Through the Eyes of a Gentile 103

Chapter 18: From Church to a Synagogue 113

CHAPTER 19:	Call of a Gentile / Learning Jewish Culture	119
CHAPTER 20:	Saved By Jesus / Walking With Yeshua	123
CHAPTER 21:	Ruth and Boaz	133
CHAPTER 22:	A Voice of Wisdom	143
Epilogue		153

Introduction

As I see my life today, I marvel at the awesomeness of God. He took someone like me, cleansed me from the inside, led me in His ways, and allowed the Holy Spirit to do His work through me. As I finish this book, my husband Rabbi Yossi Laster and I are leading a Messianic Jewish Synagogue in Lakeland, Florida. I have been walking with the Lord now for 37 years and have been in a Messianic Jewish synagogue since April 1981. After 34 years in the Messianic movement, I will attempt to bring clarification to what is happening within the Body of the Messiah—the Church.

I begin my story at the point I thought was the end of my life, without any hope and full of fear for my future. Who am I that God would choose someone like me and give me a calling in the prophesized Messianic End Times Movement? Let me tell you, it's not about me. The Word of God says:

> *Brothers and sisters, think of what you were when you were called. Not many of you were wise by human standards; not many were influential; not many were of noble birth. But God chose the foolish things of the world to shame the wise; God chose the weak things of the world to shame the strong. God chose the lowly things of this world and the despised things—and the things that are not—to nullify the things that are, so that no one may boast before Him.*
> [1 Corinthians 1:26-29]

My story has nothing to do with me, but it has everything to do with God and who He is! My prayer is that the God of Abraham, Isaac and Jacob would touch people with this story and the glory be given to Him. My hope is that other Gentiles that are being called to Messianic Judaism would find hope and better understanding of what God is doing as he calls the body of the Messiah back to its Jewish roots. As we are drawn to Yeshua, King of the Jews and Redeemer of the world, it is important that we as Gentiles understand our role in order to become the people who fulfill the Scripture: I tell my story from the beginning to show the power of God through all the cleansing I had to go through in order to get my Temple ready for the use of the Master's hand.

> *Again I ask: Did they stumble so as to fall beyond recovery? Not at all! Rather, because of their transgression, salvation has come to the Gentiles to make Israel envious.* [Romans 11:11]

We need to ask ourselves, how are we making Israel envious? What do we have they would want? How are we introducing Yeshua to the Jew?

BROKEN ROADS THAT LED ME TO YESHUA

I remember sitting at the breakfast table on a Sunday morning in the spring of 1971. I woke up feeling happy. I enjoyed cooking for my family and looked forward to sitting together for our meals. As I was about to start eating, the phone rang and a woman's voice asked, "Is this Alex's wife?"

"Yes it is," I answered.

"I'm calling to let you know your husband has been dating my sister for quite some time and I thought you should know."

I didn't want to believe what she was saying and I called her a liar. However, she knew the names of my children and also said my husband would take my youngest child with him on these dates. "If you don't believe me, go to the restaurant where she works and you can ask her yourself." She continued to tell me where this woman worked, as well as other information she thought I should know.

When I hung up the phone, I had this numb feeling and did not know what to say. I could not cry, nor did I know how to confront my husband. When my husband asked who was on the phone, I just stared at him for a moment. "That was your girlfriend's sister!" As soon as I said that, I began to cry and left the kitchen and went to my bedroom.

He followed me and asked, "What are you talking about?"

I told him what she had said, but he denied it. I knew I was about to confront my worst nightmare—the other woman!

I remember sitting on the bed crying so much I could hardly speak. I turned to my husband and asked him to tell me the truth, so I would not have to go and find out for myself. He continued to deny it and I asked him to please tell me the truth, so we could try to work this out. However, he refused and continued to deny it. I went to the kitchen, finished feeding my children, and went back to my bedroom. I had decided to go meet his girlfriend.

As I was getting ready, I remember staring at myself in the mirror and thinking, "Where did I go wrong?" All the years I had been married to my husband, I took very good care of myself. I always tried to look my best. I kept the house clean. I tried to be a good wife and a good mother. I never wanted anything else except to have a good family life. I loved my children very much and wanted them to be happy. I never drank, never smoked, and I didn't like to going to bars.

At this point in our marriage, at my husband's insistence, I was working at a finance company. He used to tell me, "You better get a job, because you never know what can happen." Now I found myself getting ready to go and meet the reason for his comment. I was about to meet my foe, my competition!

When I got to the place where she worked, she was walking in. I recognized her by the description her sister had given me. I walked up to her and asked, "Are you Jane?"

She said, "Yes."

I said to her, "I'm Alex's wife, can we talk?"

We walked outside and I asked her, "How long have you been dating my husband?"

She said almost two years. When she told me the length of time, I wanted to die. It would have been easier for me to understand it if it had been a one-time affair. She went on to tell me the only reason Alex had not asked her to marry him was because I would not give him a divorce. "He loves me so much," she said, "He even brings his son with him so that I can get to know him." She sounded so sure of what she was saying; I knew our marriage was over.

I assured her I did not know about the affair until that very morning. I told her if she wanted Alex, she could have him. After all, I had to keep a little bit of my pride. I told her, "After meeting you, you probably won't be able to find anyone else who would want to marry you. I, on the other hand, can do much better than Alex." You see, this young girl was not attractive at all. If she had been pretty, I could have somehow understood why he had done this.

The conversation ended and I got in my car and drove off. As soon as I got into my car, I burst out crying uncontrollably. I went to an isolated place to try and make some sense of it all. Again, I asked myself, "What did I do wrong?" Maybe I'm not pretty anymore or maybe I nag. I was looking for answers. I was blaming myself for what Alex had done and started thinking I just was not good enough for him. I stayed there for what seemed to be forever. I finally calmed down and started thinking of all the years Alex and I had been together.

We had been together since high school. He had been the only man I had ever loved. I began thinking I couldn't give up on my marriage so easily. I have got to fight and try to work this out. Besides, what about my children, what will happen to them? I did not want a divorce. I finally pulled myself together and went home. I thought to myself: I'll go back home and talk to my husband. He would say, "I'm sorry," and then promise never to do something like this again. However, things did not turn out the way I had hoped.

When I got home I told him I had met his girlfriend and asked him if he loved her and if he wanted to marry her. At first he wouldn't answer me, so I started crying again. The pain I felt was so intense I thought my heart was literally going to burst. I expected tenderness, sympathy, something along those lines from my husband, but he would say nothing. I continued to express my desire to make our marriage work and suggested we talk to the priest (I was a Catholic at the time). I also suggested going to other types of marriage counselors. He would not respond to any of my suggestions or comments. Instead, he had an angry look on his face. I remember saying to him, "I can't believe you're standing there, seeing how hurt I am, and instead of saying, "I'm sorry I hurt you." You're standing there with that angry look on your face."

I said to him, "At least promise me you'll never do this again and I will forgive you."

Keep in mind at this point, he had not asked for forgiveness.

I remember he gave me the ugliest look and said, "I'm not promising anything. I don't know if I'll go out on you again, thou I probably will."

He left the room, went outside, got in his car and drove off.

Needless to say, the next few months were unbearable. I kept holding my children for comfort. I was trying to sort out my thoughts and emotions. I kept thinking of what I was going to do. Several weeks went by and my husband showed no remorse for what he had done, nor did he ever say he was sorry he hurt me. All I saw was an angry look that told me he was sorry he had been caught, but not sorry he had a long-time affair. I tried talking to him on several occasions, but he was not interested. As time went on, I began to feel different and I noticed I was not hurting as much. It was as though every time I tried and he rejected, I was caring less. Since he would not talk to me about the situation or show any interest, I finally told him, "If you ever do this again, I will divorce you." He turned, looked at me and grinned.

Even though I had just threatened him with divorce, the very idea scared me to death. At the time all this happened I was working for a small finance company making very little money. I had only gotten this job because I had lied about my education. I never graduated from high school. Born into a very poor family, I lived in a two-room house in a barrio. A barrio is a poor Spanish-speaking neighborhood, full of crime and gangs.

And if this was not tough enough, there were fourteen of us in our family; my mother and father and twelve children. In a situation like this, the older kids had to drop out of school in order to help out at home. All odds were against me as far as making it on my own, much less with two children.

I was regularly attending Catholic Church and I remember praying like I had never prayed before. I was seeking God the only way I knew how at the time. I would ask him, "Why did this happen to me?" I would ask the same question every night as I cried myself to sleep. This went on for several weeks. All the while, Alex's attitude towards me remained the same. He came and went as he pleased as if nothing had happened.

One Sunday in great anguish I went to Church. All I remember is kneeling at the pew crying, but something happened to me that morning. The moment I kneeled, it seemed as though I had fallen into a trance. I saw the brightest light coming toward me and touching me. I didn't know what this was at the time and no one else saw it. It seemed as if I had only been there for a couple of minutes, but when I opened my eyes a whole hour had passed. People were already walking out of the Church. As I started out the door, I noticed an unexplainable peace and comfort, only God knew I would need in order to make it through the next few weeks.

I went home right after Church. I didn't take my boys with me that morning because I needed to be alone. At about 2 p.m., Alex got dressed and started out the door. I asked him where he was going. He just said, "Out!"

As he drove off I decided to get in my car and follow him. This was the first time in all our years of marriage I had done something like this. I drove through one of the main streets and somehow lost him. I knew more or less the area of town where his girlfriend lived so I drove towards it. There he was at her house. I started driving towards him. He saw me coming and immediately drove off.

Something really strange happened to me when I saw him there. I felt the coldest chill come over me. It was as though someone had shut off the button on my feelings. I could not cry anymore. From that moment on I hated my husband with the same strength I had once loved him. From that day on I never shed a tear for him or cared about our marriage. I decided right there and then on divorce. I was the type of person that once I made a decision, I was not changing my mind.

I went home, took all his clothes to his mother's house and called a friend from work. She and I went to a bar in Juarez, Mexico and had a Coca Cola and talked. This was the first time in my life I had done something like this. Why I did that, I still don't know. I guess my hurt, fears and the confusion I was going through, wound up in my actions making no sense. I did not stay out late. I got home around 9:00 p.m., but Alex still dared to come home about 11:00 p.m. Finding his clothes missing, we got into a big fight. He was used to me being very submissive. He always thought he could control me. I used to listen and do what he said, not because I was afraid of him, but because I loved him. I always told myself I would do anything to make my marriage work. I never wanted my children to be without a father.

From then on submissive I was not. I asked him to leave the house, but he wouldn't leave. Even at that point, he didn't show remorse or ask for forgiveness for what he did. He said to me, "If you don't like it, go file for a divorce." He didn't believe for a moment that I would ever divorce him. He knew I didn't have the education needed to get a good job. The following day I called in sick to work. I went to an attorney that had been recommended to me by my friend and I filed for a divorce. I came home and told Alex I had filed for divorce and that he had to get out of the house. He didn't believe me, so I showed him the receipt for the funds I had paid the attorney. It took a couple of weeks of intense arguing but he finally left.

I was so full of hate and I wanted to see him pay for what he had done. I was also very angry at myself for being so stupid and allowing this to happen to me. By the time we separated and during the waiting period for the divorce to be finalized, I kept thinking of how I had allowed him to control me. Nothing I ever did was good enough for him. Everything I wore was either too sexy or too childish looking. Although he had never physically abused me, he had continuously abused me verbally. Because of the verbal abuse I had become very insecure. By the time I was finally alone, and had time to think, I wasn't sure of who I was or what capabilities I had. I used to think I was dumb and ugly.

I started going to nightclubs with my friend. I remember the very first time my friend and I went to one. I got sick to my stomach as we were sitting in the car in the parking lot trying to build up enough courage to go in. I had never done something like this before. I was 26 years old at the time. Aside from being a mother of two boys, I still felt like a little girl. We never made it into the club that first time and we ended up going home. Neither one of us had the nerve to go into the club. The next time we tried, it got easier. I remember the first time I actually danced with someone else, I felt so dirty. I kept thinking of myself as a divorcee—a dirty word at time. I think divorce is a dirty and destructive word. I hated Alex more and more every time I walked into a club. What does Alex have to do with me going to clubs you might ask? I never liked to drink, and people would tell me, if I had gone to the bars with him, maybe he would have been happier. So I thought, if only I had done this before now, I would not be going through this divorce. So I was determined to change. I was going to learn to drink and have fun!

A few weeks went by and Alex realized I was going through with the divorce. He tried to talk me out of it but I didn't want anything to do with him. I came home late one night, and as I was getting out of my car, he was hiding behind a bush. He came at me with a knife, threatening to kill me if I didn't take him back. He forced me back into my car and had me drive down to a levee. He was very angry and said he did not want a divorce. He raped me at knife point. I was so scared. All I could think of was my boys. What will happen to them if Alex decided to kill me? I promised to take him back. At this point and because of all the ugliness that was going on in our marriage, I could not stay married to him. I had also dated before our divorce was final, and I was afraid to tell him.

There was no way our marriage could've worked out. He moved back in and one month later I found out I was pregnant!

The next year together was like being in hell. I hated being pregnant, not because I didn't want my baby, I just hated the fact I was pregnant by him. I was trapped for another year with this man I now hated and I had to wait on the divorce. The courts would not issue a divorce to a pregnant woman. Pregnant women were considered emotionally unstable. So I had to wait until my third child was born. Two months after my baby was born, I got a job with a good company and I filed for a divorce again. Alex moved out in August 1972 and my divorce was final February 1973. I was about to begin a chapter in my life nobody could have prepared me for in advance.

Life as a Single Parent

I started life as a single parent with three boys. My oldest, Woody (Alex) was ten years old. He was always very quiet and afraid. He was an absolutely adorable child. He was always the best at anything he set his mind on doing. However, the relationship with his father was not the best. My husband was not a person to whom you could ever express any type of feelings. He was a strong disciplinarian but lacked in showing love. He disciplined Woody in a way that was not appropriate for a ten-year-old. By the time my ex-husband was out of our lives, Woody was full of anger and fear.

My middle boy, Paul, was five years old. Paul was full of life and always had a smile on his face. Because of his type of personality, my ex-husband was able to show a little more affection to him. He missed his father and I didn't know how or what to say to comfort him. What do you say to a five-year-old when he asks, "When is dad coming home?" They just don't understand, no matter what you say.

My youngest son, Michael, being a newborn, never got to know his father. So there I was, starting my life as a single parent.

I could never have imagined what it would be like to go to work every morning and then come home every evening, to three children, who needed so much of me. At the same time, I was also trying to make some time for myself to sort out my own emotions and feelings. If this was not enough to worry about, the salary I was making was not enough to cover the expenses of rent, utilities, and baby needs, etc. My ex-husband had been ordered by the court to continue helping with child support, but he was stubborn and was not about to contribute. I took him to court on several occasions in order to make him comply, but he still continued to refuse. I hated him all the more for it, and I promised myself, somehow, I was going to make him pay. The laws concerning child support in the 1970's were not what they are today. My ex-husband finally left town and I was not financially able to pursue him for support.

So, I was forced to get a second job. I would leave the house at 7:30 a.m., work at my first job from 8 a.m. to 5 p.m., and then work at a collection agency from 6 p.m. to 10 p.m. This continued for almost two years. Even with the long work hours, I was barely paying the bills and buying enough food. I would come home exhausted every night and my children were always asleep by the time I got there. Thank God for the 16-year-old girl who was living with me at the time. I had been so busy trying to survive, that I had not taken the time to think of my future. I hardly saw my children. I had no time left to be a mother. This reality made me angry all over again.

Every time one of my children needed something, I was unable to give it to them, so I hated my ex-husband all the more. I thought to myself, "He was the cause of the divorce and there he is enjoying life without a care in the world." And here I was left with all of the responsibility. I needed money in order to pursue him on the child support issue, but I had none. I started thinking of what I could do to be able to stay home with my children. The only solution I could think of was to get married again. By this time I had built up my self-confidence and I believed in myself as a person. I found out I wasn't as dumb as my ex-husband had tried to make me feel. I had been able to maintain my family for almost two years on my own. I also realized I was attractive, as men were always asking me out. I was sure this was the best solution I could find, so I began my search for a husband and a father for my boys.

I was almost 28 years old, and I had an 11-year-old, a 6-year-old and a 1-year-old baby. How would I start dating and what would I look for? Since my ex-husband had been the only man I had ever been with, I was scared. The only thing I knew for sure was that whoever I would go out with had to accept my children. If marriage was going to be in the picture, that man would have to be willing to be a father to my boys. However, I didn't realize I was going into a different decade. I was about to find out that dating in the 1970's was not like it was in the 60's.

I started accepting dates and, for some strange reason, I was very lucky. The only type of men I would date, for the most part, were men with position and money. I was sure I was going to find a man who really loves me and wanted to take care of me and my children.

The first man I dated was an attorney. He was the sweetest and most caring man I had ever met, and he showered me with gifts. He told me he had fallen in love with me. What I didn't realize was that all the gifts and words came with the expectation of payback. After several dates, he invited me to a motel. I had been told by some friends that sex was normal for a date, so I went with him. I really liked this man and I thought maybe he was going to propose to me. I could not have been more naïve.

It was payback time for all the gifts and all he had done for me. So I paid him back. I soon learned that sex was all he wanted. He had no intention of marrying me or taking care of my children. I had been trying to be lady-like, but after this realization, I no longer felt the same about him. I began to date other men, still looking for Mr. Right, while continuing to date him. The more men I dated, the more I was finding out there was no man out there who would ever get serious about a divorced woman with three children. All men ever wanted was a good time.

I came to a place in my life where I really didn't care anymore about getting married. I found myself hating men and not wanting anything to do with them. I had also found out the attorney I was dating was married. I didn't think of asking if he was married when I met him. I just automatically assumed he was single. When I found out he was married, it made me think of my ex-husband and what he had done to me. This man had a wife at home and he thought he was going to get away with this. I started to retaliate. It seemed like the worse I treated him the more he chased me.

Every time I went out with another man, I lost more and more respect for them, as well as for myself. It became a game I liked to play. Each man became a challenge I had to conquer. I started thinking of how fun it would be to see how many I could date at the same time without any of the others finding out. To add to the fun, I refused to sleep with any of them. I noticed how all of them would give me the same lines. It was as though they had gotten together and practiced. It became a predictable routine. They would take me to dinner, buy me gifts and expect me to go to bed with them. But I now knew how the game was played, and I decided to be the winner. I took pleasure in hurting as many men as I could. It was payback time!

I no longer wanted a husband or a father for my boys. My dream of having that had died and my hope in the male race died with it. I had to come to grips with the fact men just wanted to play house, but were in no way, looking for any type of commitment or responsibility. I was more confused now than when I started dating. In my heart I longed to find a man who would love me the way I needed to be loved. I loved my boys very much, and wanted the best for them, but I had to begin to live with the fact that nobody would help me raise them.

The longer I continued dating, the colder I became. I only went out for fun and to see what I could get out of men. I made up my mind I would lead them on but there was not going to be any sex. It was so strange; when I tried being a lady, they tried taking advantage of me. There was no longer any room for weakness. Now that I was less than a lady, they chased me like flies to honey and I liked that. It meant I was in control. My heart had gotten so cold I felt nothing for any of them. This one man I had dated was very handsome and so nice to me. I wondered why I couldn't even like him.

Ironically, by this time, I had received several marriage proposals, all of which I declined. I didn't want it anymore. I knew how the game was played. I also knew, that the men who wanted to marry me, had very little or no interest in my boys. I had gotten so cold-hearted and uncaring I no longer cared if they were married or not. If they were married, I just made it a point to destroy them. With every man I hurt and left, I thought of my ex-husband. So in a sense, all of them were still paying for what my ex-husband had done to me.

I began sleeping with them. But every time I slept with a man, I did it with the intent of making them fall in love with me so I could hurt them. I was so embittered, that I could not find a man I liked, much less loved. What started out as a search for a husband had become a destructive mission.

In essence, I was a mother of three little men, who absolutely hated men. I never thought of the impact this was having on my sons until it was too late. I had lost focus on what I was trying to accomplish in life. All I had ever wanted was to be a wife and a mother. Now all I could think about was revenge on men. I could not believe how hateful I had become. I started dressing quite different on my dates and would expose a lot. I did this on purpose, just to tease. I finally got bored with what I was doing and I hated what I had become. But I felt I had to be this way in order to survive in this rotten world. I hated everything and everyone around me. As I thought of the overwhelming responsibility of raising and providing for my children, it scared me to death. Almost two years had passed since the divorce and I hardly saw my children because of the long working hours and the dating.

I finally decided to stop dating all together. I went back to just working and staying home with my children. I did this for several months and I tried to use this time to re-group and figure out how I was going to support my children. I used to get so angry when my children would ask me to buy them things they needed. I didn't know how to make them understand I couldn't afford them. I wasn't angry towards them, I was angry at the situation. How do you tell your 12-year-old you can't afford to buy him a pair of shoes or school supplies or that he can't be in sports because you can't afford his uniform? They just don't understand. When my little one wanted ice cream, I couldn't buy it. This was the sad state I was in.

One afternoon, my friend Nora called and asked me to do her a favor by going out with this certain man. At first I refused, but she was so persistent I finally agreed. I made sure to tell her it would be for this one time only. The favor she wanted was for me to go out with this guy in order to make someone else jealous. She wanted to see if I could get him away from the other-woman (more types of games people play). The other-woman had gone out with Nora's boyfriend and she just wanted to get even. Life was all about games at this point, so I either learned to play, and win, or I got wiped out. And I learned to play very well. I never used to let anybody come to my house, so I met him and Nora at a bar. He was attractive, but very prideful. He owned some business and had lots of money, but my friend had not mentioned any of this. Anyway, the only reason I was going out with him was to make his girlfriend jealous.

His name was Don and we went to dinner, had a couple of drinks, and then called it a night. I thanked him for dinner and started to leave, but he wasn't used to that kind of treatment. He followed me to my car and insisted I spend more time with him that evening, but I told him I had to go. He asked me for my telephone number, but I told him to look it up in the directory (my number was unlisted). I had become such an ugly, emotionally numb person, that even though this man was attractive and had money, I was not interested. He was as prideful and as much a jerk as all the rest. I went home that night with no intent of ever seeing him again. He was the type of man who had a woman for each night of the week. That interested me, but only because I saw a challenge. After giving it some thought, I decided against it.

My friend Nora called me at work saying Don was constantly asking her for my telephone number and she asked me if she could give it to him. I told her not to, but a couple of weeks went by and my friend called me at work apologizing. She said, "He wore me down and I gave him your number." I told her it was okay; I would take care of it. I was frustrated over the whole situation and I was really not in any mood to go through this kind of game playing. By this time in my life there was no man who could impress me, even if he had money.

Don was calling me all the time and after a couple of weeks I decided to go to dinner with him. I needed to ease the stress I was under anyway, at least that was my excuse. Quite honestly, I needed some kind of an escape to ease my emotional disappointment. I took some time to think of ways I might better myself. I thought of going back to school, but I knew those thoughts would never go beyond being just that, thoughts. The fact I was raising three children on my own, I knew there was no way I could do much more than what I was already doing. I didn't feel good about myself. The thought of being so young and having the great responsibility of raising my boys was overwhelming. Don was always trying to impress me with his money. When I decided to start dating him, it was with the intent of taking him for whatever I could. He had money anyway and I needed some. If he liked games I was ready to play. I might as well get something out of it I thought. I dated Don for several months but did not have sexual relations with him. I figured if he didn't like it he could leave. No loss for me! He would chase me, buy me, dine me and do everything he could to get me to like him.

One evening, without me knowing, he followed me home and found out where I lived. I didn't know he had done this until the following day. I got home from work and my babysitter told me a man had come to the house and said hello to my boys. Then he left and came back with a bunch of groceries. I went to the refrigerator and found it full. I looked in the cabinets, which were also full of groceries. I went to my room and started crying. I had just gotten paid, but my paycheck was all gone from paying bills and I had no money left for food. I didn't know how I would feed my children that week. When I saw what he had done it softened my heart towards him. He didn't have to do that; why would he go to that extreme? I thought, maybe, there is a man out there who was different and I finally found him.

Later that evening he called me and invited me to dinner and we went out. Don was always at my house now and the boys grew very fond of him. He was always taking us places. He started paying my bills and giving me money to help out. If the boys needed anything, he would buy it for them. I continued to date him. I felt like the weight of my financial burden had been lifted. But I noticed I had let my guard down. He now had the upper hand.

3

DECEIVED

I liked Don, but I had made up my mind I would never fall in love with him. The holidays were coming up and my boys and I shopped like we had never shopped before. For the first time in my life money was no object. However, something strange happened on the eve of the holiday. Don came over and stayed awhile and then he said he had to leave and could not come back until the morning. I asked where he was going, but he said he had to take care of something important and he would explain in the morning. He came over early the next morning and I asked him to explain. He told me his children had made him promise he would spend that evening with them. I was shocked and asked, "What children?"

Yep, he was married. We had been dating for six months and he was always with me at my house. I never would have guessed he was married. He kept on telling me he didn't love his wife. He said he loved me and did not want to lose me. So, I gave him one week to file for divorce or get out of my life. I never thought he would get a divorce. Either way, I stopped seeing him immediately. I would not talk to him on the phone nor would I go out with him on dates. Even though I had gotten to like him very much, I had become so hard of heart, that I could drop him just as quickly as I had picked him up. Anyway, he had lied to me, and I could not tolerate that. When we first started dating, I had asked him if he was married and he said he wasn't.

I didn't care if he came back; I had gotten used to disappointments. Two weeks later, I got home from work and found his suitcase in my bedroom. Later that afternoon he came over and showed me the receipt for the divorce and 60 days later he was a free man.

"Now we can move on," he said. So move on we did. He had four children and I started talking to him about them. I asked him why his children were never with him. He said they never wanted to be with him. I thought this was kind of strange because he was so wonderful to my boys. I insisted he begin a relationship with them, so he started bringing them over to my house. I immediately fell in love with them, and they with me. I noticed they were afraid of him. He was very nice to my boys but he would always yell at his children. I had a talk with him and put a stop to it. His children came over all the time now and they started wanting to spend the night.

Don and I had been living together for several months. No matter how good this man was to us, I just could not love him. I also noticed I had to be in control of every situation. He was making drastic changes. He was not as prideful as he had been when I first met him. He would do everything I would ask him to do, and I liked that. I remembered the promise I had made to myself after my divorce: No man would ever control me again! Don would do and give me anything to keep me happy, but I would not give him my heart.

Even though I had told him I had no intention of marrying, he asked would it be OK to build a bigger house for me since his children were coming over so often. Hey, a new house, how often does this happen? I was excited over the fact I would get to choose and pick what kind of house I wanted. The house was built and finished in about three months. We went to the most expensive furniture place in town and bought a whole houseful of furniture. He paid off all my bills and bought me everything I, or my boys, wanted or needed.

4

Money—The Answer

My new life began in this beautiful house with no more bills and no more financial worries. I decided to continue working because I felt if I quit my job I would be solely dependent on Don, and I was not about to let that happen. I had been through that with Alex. I was now working for a good company as an administrative supervisor, and even though I was making decent money it was still not enough to handle being a single parent with three children. He continuously asked me to stop working and stay home with the children. As much as I wanted to stay home, the fear of being totally dependent on a man again was too great.

 Don and I started going out more often, and I had a full-time maid to take care of the household chores and watch the children after school. On weekends we would barbecue and his children would come over all the time. I didn't mind. I always liked children. I started drinking more and more whenever we went out. I failed to mention this nice man had a drinking problem and he socialized with lots of friends. I became a part of this world. Don would buy me all kinds of jewelry and I bought very expensive clothes. At a certain point in our relationship I had $40,000 worth of diamond rings on my fingers and I began to get very prideful. Everybody in my family looked up to me in a sense. My mother once said, "You finally found happiness." I remember looking at her with a big smile and thinking to myself: I do have everything I could possibly want. I have absolutely no need. I have a man who will do anything I ask. He spent lots of time with my boys, playing with them and talking to them. But I'm not happy. I didn't know what was wrong with me. If I had all this, why was I not happy?

I always loved playing sports. Don had bought a boat and everybody was content. We all learned to water ski and had a great time. We would go out of town on weekends and water ski. The boys loved it and I felt very comfortable for a while. And again, I was drinking more and more as time went on. Don and I kept on going out to parties, dinner dates, and so on. All of these occasions included drinking and drugs.

At 28-years-old I became exposed to marijuana and cocaine. I didn't mind people doing drugs. I always told myself it was not my business if people wanted to ruin their lives with the stuff. But I promised myself I would never get into drugs. There is a saying: Don't play with fire or you'll get burned. Well, burned was what I got and it was more burned out!

Don and I started travelling. We went all over Mexico, Las Vegas and California. Don kept trying to make me happy by buying me things. Some men, or should I say most men, think they are showing love to a woman by doing outward things for her or by buying stuff. Although those things do have a place, a woman needs to feel loved by a gentle touch. If a man learns to do this then his wife or girlfriend will do anything to make him happy.

I noticed Don's children began depending on me more and more. They would come to me for advice and whatever else they needed. They would come to the house after school and ask for help with their homework. I also noticed Don was staying at work more than usual and I began to resent that. He began to leave me with the responsibility of dealing with my children and his children as well. I didn't mind helping with his children, but I felt he was neglecting them.

I resented the fact that Don seemed bothered when his children needed him. I began to talk to him about his neglect as a father. I also noticed Don knew how to give the children a good time, but he was far from knowing how to be a father. He didn't like the idea of me talking to him about parental issues and it began to bring a separation between us. We continued going out, and as time went on I began drinking more and more. We started arguing more about different issues. I tried talking to him about becoming more involved in real-life issues with his children, instead of him just trying to be their pal. He resented that. I had become very frustrated over the whole situation, but I decided to stick it out for a while—whatever that meant. To be honest, I looked at all the material things I had and I would get scared of the thought of going back to the way I was before I met Don.

Don came home one evening and asked to talk to me. He said someone had made him a business offer that would make us millionaires in a very short time. I asked him why he needed more money than what he already had. He said if he made this deal he could retire and begin to concentrate on a family life. I finally asked him the details. He reluctantly told me he was going to start dealing drugs. I was shocked! I tried to talk him out of it and told him I would not be a part of it. He pleaded with me and asked to please let him do this for only one year and after a year he promised he would stop. I finally gave in. I told him I would agree to exactly one year, to the day, and if he did not quit, I would leave. Even though I had agreed to these conditions, I was very scared and angry. I had no idea what all this meant. I kept thinking of how selfish he was to put us all in that kind of danger.

My Family on Drugs

He began to make different kinds of friends. Every party we attended started off with drugs and ended with drugs. I had gotten to the point in our relationship where I resented being with him. I had, once again, stopped caring. One afternoon someone offered me a marijuana cigarette and, for the first time, I took it. My life on drugs had begun.

From that day forward, I began to smoke marijuana on a daily basis. I liked the way it made me feel. It made me forget my worries and I liked that. It became a way of escape for me. And if that wasn't enough, a couple of months later I began to do cocaine.

I began to justify doing drugs. I started doing them out of anger and continued because it made me feel good. They helped me escape from the frustrations I was going through with Don; at this point, I didn't even want to be with him anymore. I was with him out of convenience now. There were times when I would stay home from work because I had been out to the wee hours of the morning having a good time. I would sit in the living room, in the sunken fireplace area, with the fireplace going. I would stare at the beautiful house which had thick high beams; I would walk into my bedroom which had white carpeting, beautiful furniture, a hot tub in our bathroom, and a double-closet full of all kinds of clothing. I would walk into my boys' bedrooms and glance at the beautiful furniture. They had their own television sets and closets full of cloths. We had a boat parked out in the driveway. We had a refrigerator full of all kinds of foods, and in the garage we had a freezer packed with lobster tails, shrimp, all kinds of steaks and more. We had just about everything anyone could possibly want but I would still go back to my bedroom and start crying. I could not figure out what was wrong with me. Why can't I be content with all this? Yes, Don had gotten into drug dealing, but for the most part, he was a nice guy. He never mistreated me or my boys. He gave us anything and everything we wanted or needed. So why was I so miserable?

The years went on without an answer, and so I continued to do more drugs. Don and I would go out, and in one evening, I would drink a fifth of Jack Daniels, smoke marijuana and sniff cocaine. There were many nights I didn't remember how I had gotten home. I guess I would pass out. All the while, Don thought this kind of behavior was funny. Things got worse between us. We argued all the time and our lives became one big party. I had started out looking for a family lifestyle with a father, mother, children, home and happiness. But it was obvious by now I was never going to find the kind of life I wanted for my children and myself.

Don's children continued coming over. However, because of the drugs, my patience with the children was not the same. I felt very jittery and anxious all the time. I could no longer get through the day without either drinking alcohol, or doing some kind of drug. My mornings started with a line of cocaine just to be able to make it to work. Then I would do a couple more of lines of cocaine during work hours in order to make it through the day. By the time I left work I was so strung out on cocaine I would immediately light a joint (marijuana cigarette) in order to calm down. My life went on like this for the remainder of my time living with Don.

Don's oldest son, Jim, brought me his report card to show me that his grades had improved from D's to B's. He was now 16, it was Easter vacation, and he came to me and asked if he could go visit his friend who had just moved to Houston. He said, "My dad said I could go if you say it's okay."

So based on his grades and the fact he missed his best friend, I said he could go. He flew to Houston on a Thursday morning. Don and I were planning to go out with the children the next day. On Friday afternoon, I had just gotten home from work when the phone rang. I answered. The voice asked, "Is this Jim's mom (Don's children used to call me mom)?"

I said, "Yes it is."

The voice said, "I have some bad news for you. Jim was in a car accident and was killed."

I gave the phone to Don and he began to talk to the person on the phone. Don's son was in a car that ran a stop sign. He was the only one killed. I began to cry bitter tears, and immediately felt responsible for his death. So many questions were running through my head: Why didn't I say no? Where was Don? Why did he send him to me?

Things got worse between us. I would argue with him all the time because even at this point when his children needed him so much, he would not talk to them at all. I was so full of hate for Don I did not want to be around him. I hated Don because he had let me down. I asked for a family life, and all he gave me was fun, possessions, and drugs—in that order.

A couple of months after Don's son's death, I was at a friend's house on a Saturday morning. We had been smoking and drinking. I went to my house to get money to go shopping. Don and I were going to a party that evening and I wanted to buy a new dress. When I got to the house, the house was empty. I walked into my bedroom, walked into my closet and started glancing at all the clothes I had. My bathroom had a beautiful sunroof. As I walked out of my closet, I stopped and looked at myself in the mirror and rearranged the skimpy crop top blouse and hot pants I was wearing. As I turned to walk away I noticed my eyes were very red. I had forgotten to use eye drops to clear the red caused from smoking. I remember thinking how evil I looked. I started turning away when I felt a hand holding my face. The hand on my face was so real, I was afraid for a moment. For the first time in a long time, I was being forced to take a good look at what I had become.

I tried to turn away but I couldn't. I continued staring at myself in the mirror. I finally stopped trying to turn away. As I looked intently I saw a couple of tears trickle down my cheeks. I had cried out of frustration or anger many times before, but this was the first time in many years that I felt hurt in my heart again.

I heard a voice ask, "Where are your children?" The voice was gentle but firm. I didn't know what was happening to me at time. It was as though I had woke up from a horrible nightmare. I thought for a moment and began to wonder where my boys were. I knew someone had said Don's ex-wife was going to take them to the movies. I didn't know for sure where they were. I made some calls to try to find out who they were with, but could not find anyone at home. I wish I could say from that point on I began doing things differently. I did have a talk with Don and told him that I was tired of this kind of life. I told him if he didn't stop with the drugs I was going to leave him. By this time he was he was sure I would never leave all he had given me. He once said to me, "Yeah, sure. You're going to leave all this and do what?"

Do what was right. What was I going to do? I was hooked on drugs. I tried to stop doing drugs a couple of times, but I couldn't.

I hated being with him, but could not figure out how I would leave and start over. I continued going out. Don had developed a cold attitude as well. He told me how ungrateful I was because after all he had done for me I showed no appreciation. Don and I were arguing all the time now. By now he could do nothing that would make me happy.

Some months passed and I was trying to figure out how to leave the situation, I was hooked on drugs and didn't have much money of my own. I had not bothered to balance my checkbook in a long time. Don and I still lived in the same house but had no type of relationship anymore. We just learned to exist in the same space.

I knew it was just a matter of time before I left the situation, I just didn't know how to go about it. I had $10,000 in the bank—all of which I had saved myself. I began to think of how to use the money to rent an apartment, buy some kind of furniture and prepare to leave the situation. I had already spoken to Don about his one-year drug dealing stint being finished. I guess I still hoped he would agree to get some kind of help for us and maybe we could work things out. But that didn't happen. I had to make a drastic decision to leave and not look back.

I rented an apartment and bought some furniture. I did not say a word to anyone. One Friday after work, I went home, got all of our clothes, a small television set for the boys and moved out of the house and into our new apartment. My poor boys were all so confused about what was happening. I told them I had to leave because of different problems Don and I were having. They didn't understand how I could pick up so abruptly and leave.

By now Alex was 15, Paul was 9 and Michael was 5, and my two eldest boys were already doing drugs. Don had no idea where I had moved. I left him a note telling him I did not want to be with him and I couldn't live this kind of life anymore. In June 1978, I found myself alone and starting over again.

6

BACK TO SQUARE ONE

My boys and I started the continuation of our lives not knowing where it was going to lead. I was back to square one! I was now hooked on drugs, my eldest was using and my middle boy was doing them occasionally. My eldest son and I fought all the time. Not only did I have the financial responsibility again, now I had a teenage boy who had lost all respect for his mother and had gotten used to the good-and-easy life money can buy. Don always made sure the kids had money. That was the way he kept them busy and away from him.

After being in the apartment for a couple of weeks I became very anxious and afraid. I was always yelling at my boys. Once again, I would get home from work and take care of dinner, do laundry, help with homework and do everything else that was needed. My need for drugs remained the same but now I had no money and no one to supply me with them .

One night after the boys had gone to sleep, I went into the bathroom and thought of suicide. I had messed up our lives and now I didn't know how to fix them. If I had not loved my children so much I would have killed myself that night. The only thing that saved me was that I would never do something like that to my children. I created the problem and somehow I would find a way to fix it.

That same night I started blaming God for my problems. I had not talked to God in many years because as far as I was concerned He was a mean God who gave no help in this life. "I didn't ask to be born I yelled at Him! Why did you kick me out of the Church?" The priest at the Church told me I could no longer participate in Church functions because I was divorced, this included taking communion. I knew when I got kicked out of the Church I was doomed for hell. Especially with the lifestyle I had just come out of. I just wanted the satisfaction of finding God and telling Him face to face what I thought of Him!

I began attending different churches by myself. I wouldn't take my boys because I didn't want them exposed to this mean God I knew. I was taught if I were good I would go to heaven, and if I were bad I would go to hell. Considering the lifestyle I was coming from, I knew I was going to hell. I continued to attend different churches. I attended a different church every Sunday. I didn't know what I expected to find. Somehow I would know Him when I saw Him "I thought." I had gone to a different denominational church six Sundays in a row. Also, Don had found out where I lived and he was trying to get me to come back.

A New Birth

In August 1978, I attended a charismatic non-denominational Church. Don found out I had started going to church. He didn't know the reason I was going. One Sunday morning he showed up at my apartment and asked if he could go with me. I told him he could come but he had to drive his own car. I didn't want him to drive up with me. The only thing I was concerned about at the time was finding God.

By the time I got to church that morning, the service had already started. As I walked into the building, I felt something leap inside my stomach. The feeling was of a baby's first move in a mother's stomach. It was strong enough to make me stop and wonder what it was. I sat down on one of the back pews. Don was right behind me, so he sat right next to me. This Church was different, I thought. They were singing and raising their hands. Though this was different, it felt good.

I was still focused on wanting to see God face to face. I wasn't there to tell Him how sorry I was for my sins. I did not expect to find mercy, love or forgiveness. I knew there was no chance of me going to heaven. I just wanted the satisfaction of telling God what I thought of Him. With all my hate, I sat there waiting for something, though I didn't know what. The worship in song continued as I sat there. I felt something in this place I had never felt before. As the music continued, people were asked to come up for prayer. I did not understand what was happening. As people came back to their seats, they were crying. I thought for sure they had been told something bad. After all, this God was strict and mean. No one could ever be good enough for Him.

The music stopped and the pastor began to speak about a man named Jesus. All the years I had attended Church, no one had ever told me the man carrying the cross had a name. I used to ask who the man on the cross was, I was always told "God". I never knew God had a Son. He went on to say; God loves us so much He sent his Son, Jesus, to die for our sins. He said, "If any of you out there need help, if your life is a mess, Jesus wants you to know if you put your trust in Him, He will take your life and make something beautiful of it."

As I was sitting in the pew, I thought: "Yeah, I dare you Jesus, whoever you are. Try to take this useless life and make something good out of it." As soon as I thought that, I felt heat at my feet. I immediately looked down expecting to find something to explain it, but there was nothing. However, the heat continued to fill me and I realized what was taking place was happening on the inside. I was terrified! I thought, "Oh no, now I've really done it." I thought God was going to kill me right there and then. When the heat filled me all the way to my head, I began to cry. I did not understand what was happening. All I knew was God had touched me. The pastor kept on talking about Jesus and His love for the sinner. At the end of the service he asked for a show of hands if you decided to give Jesus a chance with your life. I remember raising my hand, but not high because I didn't want anyone to know what had happened to me. I walked out of that place born again, knowing all my sins had been forgiven by Jesus. I remember walking out of there feeling so light on my feet. I thought I was floating. I was hoping it was real but I was afraid I was having a head-rush (drug related).

As I walked out I could hear the leaves moving gently as the summer breeze passed through. I could hear the chirping of birds. It was as though I was experiencing creation for the first time. I was seeing creation with different eyes. It was a beautiful feeling. What I did not know was that God wanted to love me, not punish me. I did not know exactly what had happened to me, but for the first time in my life I did not feel like I was carrying the world on my shoulders.

This was my first encounter with God and it started with being "born again". I didn't realize this was the beginning of a new life. I told Don I needed to take a drive by myself so I went and found an isolated spot in the desert, sat in my car, starred at the sky and cried a lot. Once I stopped crying

I began to think about what had happened to me in the church. I wasn't sure what had happened, but one thing I was certain of was that GOD HAD TOUCHED ME. I was in the desert for couple of hours. I went home and Don was waiting for me. I had promised him I would give him an answer about moving back with him after we got back from Church. I told him I had decided to follow Jesus, and even though I didn't know what that meant, I wasn't going back with him. He got very upset and left. The next day I went out and bought a Bible and my new life began.

8

MAKING THE TEMPLE READY FOR GOD

I began to read my Bible every chance I got. I started by reading the Gospel of John, where Yeshua declared:

Yeshua replied, "Very truly I tell you, no one can see the kingdom of God unless they are born again." [John 3:3]

"You should not be surprised at my saying, 'You must be born again.'" [John 3:7]

Yeshua goes on to say flesh gives birth to flesh and the Spirit gives birth to the spirit. So I was born again in August 1978. The Spirit of God had just given birth to my spirit.

The way God chose to touch me that first day at Church is not the way he chooses for everyone. Being born again is a life that begins with learning how to live by faith and to learn to trust our Heavenly Father. That Sunday when I received the Lord into my heart, I felt a love I had never experienced. I went to Church looking for God in order to yell at Him and tell Him off. But God did not hear my words; He saw my broken heart. He saw a heart that was unable to love or be loved. Satan is our enemy and he makes sure to destroy as many lives as he can. But Yeshua has come to be our great healer.

At that point I could only see God as someone who forgave me. Though I didn't understand His forgiveness at the time, He gave it to me. The reason I was so angry at God was because I felt I had always tried my best to make a good life for myself and those around me. But it had been one thing after another: growing up in a Barrio (getto) being so poor, never finishing high school, and getting pregnant at 16 just to get out of my house—the list goes on.

I blamed God for my life. I used to tell Him: "I didn't ask to be born. If my life is going to be like this, you might as well kill me." Life was no longer worth living. I had tried everything and nothing had worked. Things went from bad to worse. It was hard to start my Christian life. The very first thing I had to learn was to trust Yeshua with my life. Trust was one of my weaknesses because up to this point, everyone I had ever trusted for help or comfort had let me down.

As I continued to read my Bible, I began to learn more about Yeshua. I learned He died on the cross because He loved me so much. I never had anyone love me like that before. When I came to the Lord I was full of sin, hurt and resentment. I began to talk to Yeshua all the time. I would read the Bible and try to do what it said. Every time I tried, I failed. I promised Yeshua I was going to do exactly what His word said. I also told Him if I was going to do that I also expected Him to keep his word. I didn't understand this born-again life. I still spoke to Yeshua the same way I spoke to everyone else. When I was born again, I was only a baby, spiritually- speaking. I had to learn what this life was about and how to live it. When a baby is born, the most important thing a baby needs is love. The baby has to feel loved. The next thing the baby learns is trust. As parents give their baby a bottle when it's feeding time and change the baby's diapers, the baby begins to learn trust. The baby will be burped until he/she learns to burp on his or her own and so on.

That's the way it was with the Lord. I used to attend Bible studies and everybody would tell me how I needed to claim the Word of God. There is some truth to this statement, but until you learn what you are doing and how God is in control of every situation, there can be a lot of discouragement and lots of people give up. A lot of baby believers give up on God because of a lack of understanding. When a baby is born, no parent would consider giving a baby a steak to chew on instead of milk to drink. He has to slowly develop the stomach and learn to digest. That's the way we have to learn with the Lord.

When I gave my life to Yeshua, I was still hooked on drugs. I was desperate to change. Because of the choices I had made, my whole family was in trouble. I wanted so much to believe God was real and He was my answer. I remember telling Him I would do my best (whatever that meant) to follow him, but I expected Him to be real to me as well. I did not want to go through this life by myself anymore.

9

GOD MY DELIVERER

The pressure between my job, household duties and the raising of my children was still too much for me to handle on my own. Raising children was never meant to be a one-parent responsibility. My oldest son was still doing drugs and was constantly arguing with me.

One afternoon I got home from work and the boys wanted to do something or go somewhere. I could understand their need. They were home alone—all day unsupervised—and eating a lonely lunch. They were always alone. Even with every good intention, the demand on a single parent is just too much.

I began to feel very jittery and anxious again. My body started craving drugs and my neck would hurt so much it felt as though my head was going to separate from my shoulders. I was yelling at my boys continuously. That afternoon my sister Mary called and invited us for pizza. Christy, her daughter, wanted us to join them so she could play with my sons Paul and Michael. I asked my sister to take the boys so I could have some time alone. I was home alone feeling very anxious, and I was pacing the floor once again needing drugs. I went to the phone two or three times to call Don to bring me something, any kind of drug would do, but I would immediately hang up the receiver. "I can't do this; he's going to laugh at me," I thought. I told him I was going to follow Yeshua because He had promised to change my life and He was also going to take care of my boys. So I couldn't call. Instead I went to my bedroom, sat down on my bed and started crying again. I seemed to do a lot of crying now. I started feeling let down again. I looked up and started yelling at Yeshua and calling Him a liar. I told Him, "You promised if I gave my life over to You, You would change it and help me, I still have my drug problem and you are doing nothing about it!"

I kept on crying uncontrollably, clinging tightly to the bedpost, fearing He would not show up and asking Him to please help me! I kept yelling, "If You don't help me, I have no one else to turn to for help." All of a sudden I felt a presence in my bedroom as though a cloud had covered me. The Lord's presence was so strong. I stopped crying and all my pains were gone. I stopped shaking and I no longer felt the stress. My Yeshua had come right into my bedroom and delivered me from drugs.

> Isaiah 42:7 tells us that He came *"…to open eyes that are blind, to free captives from prison and to release from the dungeon those who sit in darkness."* Isaiah 49:9 *"to say to the captives, "Come out," and to those in darkness, "Be free!" "They will feed beside the roads and find pasture on every barren hill."*

Sometimes we tend to depend so much on our pastors or friends we miss out on having our relationship with the Lord becoming more real every day.

> *Godly sorrow brings repentance that leads to salvation and leaves no regret, but worldly sorrow brings death.* [2 Corinthians 7:10]

God wants us to always come to him first. He is the only one who can deliver us from all of our troubles, whether our troubles are emotional, mental, drug related or physical. I thank God for the love and patience He has towards us.

> *The Spirit of the Sovereign Lord is on me, because the Lord has anointed me to proclaim good news to the poor. He has sent me to bind up the brokenhearted, to proclaim freedom for the captives and release from darkness for the prisoners…* [Isaiah 61:1]

And free I was! It has now been 35 years since that one day in my bedroom, and I have never touched or desired any type of drug since. Praise the Lord! I want to encourage all of my brothers and sisters in the Lord. If anything has you in bondage such as drugs, including over- the-counter drugs, cigarettes, coffee or uncontrollable sexual desires, seek the Lord He desires to set you free. I don't think there is anything wrong with a cup of coffee as long as you can start the day with or without it. We need to be in control of all we do. There are some people who can't survive without drinking coffee or having a cigarette. If you are one of these people, maybe this is the time Yeshua is asking you to come to him to be delivered. Anything that masters you is in control of you.

The end of all things is near. Therefore be alert and of sober mind so that you may pray. [1 Peter 4:7]

If we are truly born again, we must never forget why this born-again experience happened.

For those God foreknew He also predestined to be conformed to the image of His Son, that He might be the firstborn among many brothers and sisters. And those He predestined, He also called; those He called, He also justified; those He justified, He also glorified. [Romans 8:29-30]

Do not conform to the pattern of this world, but be transformed by the renewing of your mind. Then you will be able to test and approve what God's will is—His good, pleasing and perfect will. [Romans 12:2]

Before I knew the Lord I had to do a line of cocaine to get started in the morning. Now I ask you: Can you start your day without a cup of coffee or without smoking a cigarette? The Church is full of people who are hooked on these types of drugs. Sometimes we tend to only see sin as society sees it, the outward, horrible sins such as illegal drugs, alcohol and prostitution. We take notice of people who use foul language and so on. How about over-eating, gossip, judging others and many more areas in our lives? These are also addictions. These attributes define who we are. Take a moment with the Lord regarding these things. The good news is Yeshua wants to set you free, just like He did for me. Praise the Lord! He loves us so much. He gets jealous when we turn to anyone or anything else for relief. He wants to heal and restore every area of our lives. After all, we were saved to be conform to His image.

10

Expecting Quick Miracles

After Yeshua delivered me from drugs, I began to feel like my old self, whatever that meant at this point in my life. My boys and I started going to Church every Sunday and attending a Bible study class during the week. It was hard to get my oldest son to go to Church with me. I had to force him to do what I said, so he went with me. The reason I used to force him to come to Church was because I knew his only hope for healing was Yeshua. My boys had lost all respect for me as their mother, and the guilt I was carrying for destroying their lives was unbearable. After all, I was the one who got them started on drugs. As parents we all need to sit before the Lord so He can change us into His image. We make so many mistakes that affect our children. We need to learn to apologize to our children and take responsibility for our wrong doings. Being a parent is not easy. Even when we do our best, we make mistakes. However, God promises to make the crooked things straight.

I started meeting other born-again people in church and they seemed to be nice, and I thought maybe someone would help me with my boys. My boys needed to be around a man. Woody went through puberty probably not knowing what was happening to him, and I on the other hand didn't even know he was experiencing changes. All I knew was he was driving me crazy. One day he acted like a child, the next day he acted mature. I didn't know how to help him. I asked around to see if there was some kind of program for kids from divorced homes, but there wasn't. I became very discouraged. I thought of all places where I could find some kind of help for my boys would be in the church. I didn't expect the church to fix my problems.

I just needed help with my boys. The kind of help I was looking for was a role model for my sons. I wanted them to have a male influence in their lives, someone they could relate to. Still, to this date, the same void remains in the church. In the year 2014, the church continues to operate with the same mentality as it had years ago. There used to be complete families back then, meaning: father, mother and children.

Today, single-parent homes continue to grow. We have developed programs and activities for families and singles, but there remains a void for the single-parent dilemma. The church needs to look for ways to help these children get healed and prepared for the Lord's work. There are a lot of singles in the church who can provide some kind of support towards boys and girls from single-parent homes. We all go to Church on Saturdays or Sundays, listen to the teachings, do the praise and worship and then go home. For the rest of the week most people sit at home very comfortable without a thought of how they can be used in someone else's life. If one has a complete family, meaning father, mother and children, I think it would be great to include a boy from a single parent home to spend time with that family. There are different groups that try to do this kind of work outside a church setting. I believe it's the Lord's will we all take a good look at our single-parent homes and work towards keeping our children in the Lord.

My boys grew up with so many needs that could've been met by young men in the church if only they had been trained to reach out to these children.

> *Be devoted to one another in love. Honor one another above yourselves. Never be lacking in zeal, but keep your spiritual fervor, serving the Lord. Be joyful in hope, patient in affliction, faithful in prayer. Share with the Lord's people who are in need. Practice hospitality.* [Romans 12:10-13]

I needed a Godly man to have some interest in my sons for the sake of healing. Again, I went to the person leading the Bible study and shared my problems with them, and asked if there was someone who could take the time to talk to my boys. By the expressions I was getting, I knew they didn't understand how to deal with my boys or me. When they heard we were coming out of a drug lifestyle they sort of frowned upon us. You have to understand these people have been church-goers almost all their lives. I don't believe they meant to frown; they just were not prepared to deal with a single parent or drug issues. They did ask me for my phone number, and said if they found someone who could help they would give me a call. Time passed but no one contacted me.

I continued praying and reading my Bible. Then I expected to go to church and find people doing exactly what it said, but not so. The Bible study I first attended was directed towards a family setting. I thought that's where I belong because I had a family. I felt so out of place because everyone there had complete families, meaning husband, wife and children. I was a woman with children. After a month or so I began to feel out of place, and so did my boys. I used to see the longing in their eyes when the families would plan camping trips and it was only for fathers and sons. My boys were not invited, and since they didn't have a father, they never got to go. I finally left that setting and began to attend another Bible study group.

I thought maybe this group would be different. It was mainly for singles, meaning no children and never been married. I remember the first time I attended. I didn't take my boys because I knew it was for singles. When I walked in, there was silence. I felt so out of place and unwanted. You need to remember I came into the church from the filth of the world, so I was still wearing my tight jeans and false eyelashes. However my thoughts were different. I was no longer looking for a man, but I was still looking for help for my boys. However, this group didn't know the first thing about reaching out to children, much less to teen boys with drug problems. I continued with this group because I didn't know where else to go. I couldn't find anyone who truly accepted me. I couldn't make a female friend. I guess they felt threatened because of the way I looked.

> *On his arrival, Yeshua found that Lazarus had already been in the tomb for four days.* [John 11:17]

> *"Take away the stone," He said. "But, Lord," said Martha, the sister of the dead man, "by this time there is a bad odor, for he has been there four days."* [John 11:39]

I had been in my spiritual tomb for 32 years, so I'm sure I not only smelled bad, but also still looked like someone whom you would not find in the church. So in a way I sort of understood their response to me. When Yeshua called me out of my grave I, as Lazarus, was wrapped with strips of linen and a cloth around my face.

> *When He had said this, Yeshua called in a loud voice, "Lazarus, come out!" The dead man came out, his hands and feet wrapped with strips of linen, and a cloth around his face. Yeshua said to them, "Take off the grave clothes and let him go."* [John 11:43-44]

At this point I needed the people of God to help me take off my grave cloths.

In 1978 I received Yeshua as my Lord and Savior; however, at the time of my spiritual birth I could only embrace Yeshua as my Savior. He had forgiven me of my sins and had allowed me entrance into heaven by His atoning blood. People kept telling me I needed to do this or that, in other words, they meant if I was truly a believer I would not be dressing and looking the way I did. I began to feel discouraged, as I was not accepted by people. Though I knew Yeshua had accepted me and had forgiven me, others kept judging me for my past. While all of this was taking place, I hung on to this verse:

> *But God demonstrates His own love for us in this: While we were still sinners, Messiah died for us.* [Romans 5:8]

It takes time for a new believer to grow. When you're born again that is exactly what happens, you're a baby. Coming from a world of evil and hurt just like a newborn, I could only respond to love. I spent a lot of time in the presence of my Lord just to feel His love. You have to be allowed time to grow into maturity. I experienced so much rejection in Bible study groups that I was ready to give up going to church altogether. Sometimes I still see the same kind of attitude from church people towards those who come in and have not yet been saved. We need not forget our Lord's words when the question was asked:

When the teachers of the law who were Pharisees saw Him eating with the sinners and tax collectors, they asked His disciples: "Why does He eat with tax collectors and sinners?" On hearing this, Yeshua said to them, "It is not the healthy who need a doctor, but the sick. I have not come to call the righteous, but sinners." [Mark 2:16-17]

Therefore, rid yourselves of all malice and all deceit, hypocrisy, envy, and slander of every kind. Like newborn babies, crave pure spiritual milk, so that by it you may grow up in your salvation, now that you have tasted that the Lord is good. [1 Peter 2:1-3]

And I had tasted that my Lord was good. But again I was just a baby. I needed someone to nurture me in the Lord.

Accept the one whose faith is weak, without quarreling over disputable matters. [Romans 14:1]

And we urge you, brothers and sisters, warn those who are idle and disruptive, encourage the disheartened, help the weak, be patient with everyone. [1 Thessalonians 5:14]

As a baby in the Lord, all I needed was for people to be patient with me and teach me by example, not by word. As the people of God, we make this mistake so often: Someone new comes into the church and right away we tend to judge them by the way they look instead of thanking God for sending another one of His children into our fold. We need not forget all of us came from a world where Satan is considered the prince.

"Now is the time for judgment on this world; now the prince of this world will be driven out." [John 12:31]

All who come in are coming from the world, and Satan has done a good job at destroying them. It is our job to nurture these newborn babies in the Lord. It is so important that we learn the unconditional love of God as described in the Bible.

Love is patient, love is kind. It does not envy, it does not boast, it is not proud. It does not dishonor others, it is not self-seeking, it is not easily angered, it keeps no record of wrongs. Love does not delight in evil but rejoices with the truth. It always protects, always trusts, always hopes, always perseveres. [1 Corinthians 13:4-7]

The Scriptures goes on to tell us everything else will be done away with, but love will never fail.

I got to a point where I thought I would never be able to live this Christian life. My boys and I were still living at the apartment and I was struggling with finances. Again, the salary I was making was not enough to support a boy in high school, a son in intermediate school and a child in the first grade. I could not understand why I was still going through some of the same things as before. People at the church would tell me to pray for finances and boy did I pray for them. But it seemed the more I prayed, the worse it got. Did this mean God didn't love me? It got so bad that I ended up moving in with my sister Mary. She was also a single parent with three children. I brought my furniture and made her garage into a bedroom, and it became home for all of us.

MAMA LUKE

I began to doubt God's love for me because the people at the Sunday church I attended made it seem so easy. Why were my prayers not answered? I would cry a lot. As I was going through all these doubts about God's love for me, Don started coming over again offering me money. He would show me $100 bills and tell me what a fool I was for leaving all he had provided for me. He would point at me and laughing, he would ask "Where is your Yeshua now?"

I was embarrassed because I was living in my sister's garage. As new believers we need to remember there will be a cleansing and testing in every area of our lives where God wants to reveal himself. Though Mary was kind enough to allow me to move in with her, she also had a family of her own. The garage-bedroom was where my sons Paul, Michael and I slept. My sister never told me I had to sleep in the garage; it just worked out that way. Alex slept on the sofa in the living room. I went through a lot of humbling during these times. Alex was very embarrassed with the situation, though I never thought of it at the time. Mary was always very sweet to all of us. I thank God for her and every day continued to pray God's blessings upon her and her children.

I continued to seek God and read my Bible daily. It got to be so crowded at my sister's neither one of us had much privacy. If I wanted to spend time alone with the Lord I would drive out to the desert to cry all I needed. I would cry to the Lord and ask Him, "Why am I going through all this? Where did you go?" I felt so alone at times I just wanted to give up. I didn't understand. I pleaded with the Lord to help me understand what was going on. I had reached a point in my Christian walk where I had given up going to church because I just couldn't get the right answers. It was also very hard to make friends at church. I just simply felt alone again.

I listened to a Christian radio station every day on my way home from work. This one afternoon I heard a woman and a man talking about a homosexual ministry. Right away I thought of a certain young man who I had met through Don. Even though he was a homosexual, I loved this person. He was one of the nicest people I had ever met. These two people were talking about being dedicated to helping homosexuals. I wrote down the telephone number and when I got home I called. A lady answered, I told her I wanted to give them the name and number of my friend so someone would contact him. She took down the information and then asked how I was doing with Yeshua. Even though she took me by surprise, I told her I was already saved and was doing just fine. She said, "Oh yeah, then why is your heart so discouraged?" I went blank for a moment, I couldn't answer. I was shocked at the fact she knew what I was going through. She also asked if I would come see her. At first I said, "No," but she was very persistent and I could tell she was concerned about me. I finally agreed to meet her.

The place where we met was called "The El Paso Hotline." It was an outreach to all kinds of people, especially street people (drug addicts, prostitutes, etc.). They met on Friday evenings, so I went and took my children with me. When I got there I noticed there were all kinds of people. There were families meaning: father, mother and children. And there were single parents with children and singles as well. I was kind of scared because I didn't know anyone there and knew very little about this place. I asked for "Mama Luke," as she had identified herself to me. Much to my surprise, I was pointed to a small black lady sitting on a bench.

I mentioned the fact she was black because I was prejudice to blacks at the time. I almost turned to leave, but she had already seen me and was waving and signaling me to come see her. I walked towards her and she insisted I sit down next to her, so I did. The meeting had not yet started, but she turned to me and said, "I'm going to pray for you." I turned to look at her and could say nothing. The moment she began to pray for me I started crying. I remember her saying to me Yeshua knows all you have being going through, He wants you to know there is a purpose for all your sufferings, and don't worry about your boys anymore. He has become their Father and promises to bring them back to Himself and to you. He wants you to stop feeling guilty for your boys being on drugs. When she said these things it was as though my heart had burst open and a quick operation had taken place. That is exactly what I was feeling. I was carrying so much guilt for the kind of lifestyle I had led those years. I blamed myself for the way my boys had been destroyed. She asked me to bring my boys to her so she could pray for them. I called the boys over and she began to pray Yeshua would heal their little hearts and take all the confusion away from their minds. My boys also started crying and I could see Yeshua was starting to heal all of us.

The meeting started and people began to praise the Lord. Then a prayer time began afterward. I saw people being prayed for in a way I had not seen before. There was a presence there that reminded me of the time Yeshua had come right into my bedroom and delivered me from drugs. At this point I was about a 1-year-old in the Lord. I was overwhelmed by the love and acceptance these people showed towards my boys and me. Next to Yeshua, Mama Luke became the most important person in my life. She was one of the few people of God who demonstrated such unconditional love as the Bible describes. She became my spiritual mother, and we became very close. I grew to love her and her two daughters, Sissy and Cheryl, very much. By the way, she was also a single parent. Mama Luke was responsible for my training in the Lord. She always reminded me to go to the Lord before I went to anyone else for help. Her testimony was, she had been diagnosed with cancer and was sent home by her doctors because there was no hope for her. She was sent home to die. Yeshua healed her and allowed her to live until her children were grown, which was her prayer. She is now with the Lord.

Again, we need to understand God's purpose for this born-again request given to us in order to enter heaven through the shed blood of precious Yeshua. There is a bigger picture to understand who we are to become and why. We are born again for the sole purpose of being continuously conformed to the likeness of Yeshua so God will be able to accomplish His purpose for our lives and in turn be able to use us in His plan for the salvation of the world.

And we know that in all things God works for the good of those who love Him, who have been called according to His purpose. For those God foreknew He also predestined to be conformed to the image of His Son, that He might be the firstborn among many brothers and sisters. [Romans 8:28-29]

I remember messing up all the time, but Mama Luke continued to love me and encourage me to go on with the Lord. She would always say, "That's all right, baby. Just get up and try again." By what people were telling me I should've been prospering in the Lord by now, whatever that meant. Here in America people will say: "The Lord needs to bless me." They are really saying they have financial or material needs. Although there is nothing wrong with these things, the Scripture speaks of spiritual blessings and very seldom mentions material gain.

"Do not store up for yourselves treasures on earth, where moths and vermin destroy, and where thieves break in and steal. But store up for yourselves treasures in heaven, where moths and vermin do not destroy, and where thieves do not break in and steal. For where your treasure is, there your heart will be also." [Matthew 6:19- 21]

"So do not worry, saying, "What shall we eat?" or "What shall we drink?" or "What shall we wear?" For the pagans run after all these things, and your heavenly Father knows that you need them. But seek first His kingdom and His righteousness, and all these things will be given to you as well." [Matthew 6:31-33]

I kept on living in my sister's garage, my financial situation did not seem to be getting any better and the struggles with my children seemed to be the same. I would ask Mama Luke about my unanswered prayers, and she would look at me and encourage me by telling me to learn to wait on the Lord. Learn to sit in His presence and find out what it is you are to learn through all of this. Waiting isn't something anyone likes to do. We are so used to quick stops, fast food, microwave ovens and quick fixes for our problems. And if things don't get done, or happen in our timing, we either get out of the relationship or try to make something happen the way we want it to go. We always expect microwave miracles.

> *Even youths grow tired and weary, and young men stumble and fall; but those who hope in the Lord will renew their strength. They will soar on wings like eagles; they will run and not grow weary, they will walk and not be faint.* [Isaiah 40:30-31]

Sometimes I would leave the prayer meetings still doubting God in my situation. I used to think maybe God didn't love me anymore, because if He did why is He letting me go through so much? Mama Luke told me to go home and study the Book of James in the Bible; however, I didn't get into studying James until sometime later. The reason I kept putting it off was I didn't quite believe Mama at the time. I didn't believe I had to wait. I figured if God were going to answer my prayers, He would do it immediately. He was a big God and He can certainly work fast. After all, He created the world in six days and rested on the seventh. I was so used to getting my way now, it was hard for me to wait on God. I used to tell God, "You need to answer my prayers because people are watching and I'm telling them about you. So you need to come through for me."

My prayers to God went something like this: "Yeshua, now that I've decided to follow You, please give me a better house than the one I had when I was living with Don because I've told him that You were going to provide my needs and beyond. Also, please save my boys so people will see You are real. My finances need to be put in order, so please send me some money from somewhere. And do a miracle or something so I can show people what You have done for me." All my prayers had to do with me, and getting blessed and how it would make me look and feel.

One afternoon I was driving home from work listening to a Christian radio station. The pastor who was giving the message was talking about walking with the Lord even when we don't see our prayers answered. To this day I remember the exact words. He said, "Yeshua has a question for all of you listening. 'Will you follow Me if I never give you anything else?'" I felt as if a knife had just pierced my heart. I felt so bad. I had not realized my time with the Lord was always spent asking Him for things. I didn't go home right away. I went and parked at the desert area where I used to go spend my quiet times. By the time I got there I was sobbing. I apologized to the Lord for having been so selfish and self centered in my prayers. It was at this point I was going to begin to learn about suffering and its purpose, which is very Scriptural. It's not that God wasn't concerned about my needs, but if He had answered my prayers at the time I was asking, I would never have gotten to know Him the way I know Him now.

So I began to study the book of James.

Consider it pure joy, my brothers and sisters, whenever you face trials of many kinds, because you know that the testing of your faith produces perseverance. Let perseverance finish its work so that you may be mature and complete, not lacking anything. If any of you lacks wisdom, you should ask God, who gives generously to all without finding fault, and it will be given to you. But when you ask, you must believe and not doubt, because the one who doubts is like a wave of the sea, blown and tossed by the wind. That person should not expect to receive anything from the Lord. Such a person is double-minded and unstable in all they do. [James 1:2-8]

Unstable I was. I began reading the Bible with different eyes. As I read I realized there were many Scriptures relating to suffering. Before I could embrace the suffering aspect of my walk with the Lord, I needed to be given a new heart and that could only happen in the presence of God.

"I will sprinkle clean water on you, and you will be clean; I will cleanse you from all your impurities and from all your idols. I will give you a new heart and put a new spirit in you; I will remove from you your heart of stone and give you a heart of flesh. And I will put My Spirit in you and move you to follow My decrees and be careful to keep My laws." [Ezekiel 36:25-27]

The Holy Spirit is the clean water we as believers are cleansed with after we receive Yeshua as our Savior. The precious blood Yeshua shed on the cross makes atonement for all impurities that are so much a part of which we are when we come to the Lord. When I came to the Lord, I definitely had a heart of stone. I cared very little about people and I always found ways to get even with those who caused me problems or pain. I delighted in getting even. I was full of hate towards so many people. I realized I really needed a heart of flesh. Until I could rid myself of all my impurities (like wanting new things, hating people, wanting to get even and wishing wrong to others, plus all my idols like money, children, cars, houses and all other wants), I could not be used as a vessel for the Lord . By ridding myself of these impurities, I would, in turn, be able to recognize the voice of my Lord. I was about to find out the cost of following Yeshua.

The above Scripture ends with: *"And I will put My Spirit in you and move you to follow My decrees and be careful to keep My laws."* We need to understand it's only by the power of the Holy Spirit we are able to follow the Lord. It is in yielding the area of which the Lord is convicting us that He is able to heal and change us from the inside. Before I could accept the breaking of my pride and the teaching of discipline I was going to go through, I had to know—without a doubt—God loved me and everything from here on was going to be orchestrated by His hand for my life. If you never learn the reality of God's love in your life, you can't trust him with your future.

I couldn't trust someone I didn't really know. I definitely needed to know my Heavenly Father in order to trust Him.

12

SIN DESERVING DEATH

The teachers of the law and the Pharisees brought in a woman caught in adultery. They made her stand before the group and said to Yeshua, "Teacher, this woman was caught in the act of adultery. In the Law Moses commanded us to stone such women. Now what do you say?" They were using this question as a trap, in order to have a basis for accusing Him.

But Yeshua bent down and started to write on the ground with His finger. When they kept on questioning Him, He straightened up and said to them, "Let any one of you who is without sin be the first to throw a stone at her." Again He stooped down and wrote on the ground.

At this, those who heard began to go away one at a time, the older ones first, until only Yeshua was left, with the woman still standing there. Yeshua straightened up and asked her, "Woman, where are they? Has no one condemned you?"

"No one, sir," she said.

"Then neither do I condemn you," Yeshua declared. "Go now and leave your life of sin." [John 8: 3-11]

About eight months after I had been born again, I received a letter from the FBI requesting a meeting with me regarding drug issues from my past life. Even though I never sold drugs I was guilty of the crime by association. I lived with Don for about 5½ years and he was selling drugs the last two years I was with him. I went to meet with the FBI agents and was told Don had been arrested and I had to appear in court to testify about all that went on while we had been together. The agent told me he didn't know the total legal implication on my end.

I left his office and was crying on the way to my car. I was so scared. The way the agent described things to me it sounded like I would have to serve time in jail. Three weeks later I was to appear in court to tell about my involvement and to testify against Don.

I told Mama Luke what happened and she asked some ladies to fast and pray for the next couple of weeks until the date of the court hearing. During this time I prayed and fasted exactly as the Scripture requires, and the Lord had me assume responsibility for my actions and totally surrender to His will in this matter. I couldn't see a way out of this mess.

On the day of the hearing I got to the courthouse about one hour before I was supposed to be there. I was so scared I didn't want to take any chance of being late. The elevator was not working that morning. There was a janitor at the end of the hallway and he pointed me to the stairway and said, "Good morning. Don't worry; everything is going to be OK." I looked at him and thanked him.

I went up to the third floor and was told to wait in the hallway. I waited for what seemed like forever. All of the sudden, I heard this voice again. It was the same janitor and now he was mopping the end of the hallway on the third floor. He again said to me, "Try not to be afraid, everything will be fine." Again, I said, "Thank you."

I thought that was nice of him to try to encourage me, but I didn't believe things would be fine. I thought for sure I was going to be sent to jail. Don was not just a street dealer. He dealt with the Mexican Cartel. That's why I had decided to leave him. I didn't want that kind of life. But since he had gotten caught, and the charges included the years I lived with him, I was part of the situation.

After waiting in the hallway for a long time, I was called into the courtroom. The two FBI agents were with the prosecutor. They called my name and I went up front. The court had assigned me an attorney because I didn't have money to hire one. He went up with me, and was standing there with me, waiting for the prosecutor or the FBI agent to start questioning me. After a few minutes without a single question, the judge asked the prosecutor what the problem was and why there was a delay. The prosecutor told the judge they could not find my paperwork and asked the judge for more time. The judge said they could have another minute and no more. I was standing there trembling, I was so scared. I looked over to where the FBI and prosecutor were and I could see they were shuffling papers. The judge finally asked them why I was there. They told him I had taken part in the dealings regarding this trial and they wanted to have me testify. The judge got upset with them and told them since they had no paperwork for me; he had no choice but to dismiss me. The judge turned to me and said, "You are dismissed."

I asked, "Do I have to come back."

He said, "No, you are dismissed of all charges, you may go."

The attorney escorted me to the hall and said to me, "I don't know what happened in there, but you are free to go."

I walked downstairs crying tears of joy. Through a whirlwind of emotions, I thanked the Lord. If I had not been in a courthouse, I would have kneeled right then and there to give Him thanks. I left the building, and as I was walking down the stairs, I was still thanking the Lord for what He had done. As I reached the last step, I heard a voice say, "I told you everything would be OK." I turned around and there was the same janitor. He was sitting on a ledge on the side of the courthouse.

I again said, "Thank you so much," but this time with a smile on my face. As I turned away, I suddenly felt this indescribable peace and I realized the janitor was the Lord. I immediately turned back to say something else to Him, but He was gone.

> *"He will call on Me, and I will answer him; I will be with him in trouble, I will deliver him and honor him. With long life I will satisfy him and show him My salvation."* [Psalm 91:15]

As I write this and remember the miracles I've experienced, and the reality of the word of God, I can't help but think about how so many times, we tend to get angry at God for unanswered prayers. I had to learn it wasn't

God's fault I was in trouble. If I had to do time in jail it was my fault for choosing that kind of life. We need to know how to pray when we come into the presence of this so precious and Holy God. Yes, I had found out how much He loves me. I know how awesome He is and that He is able to make the crooked things straight in our lives. But you know something? We need to know He doesn't owe us all He gives and does for us. His love is so unconditional that He doesn't give us what we truly deserve.

To this day I don't know what happened in that courtroom. All I know is that Yeshua was with me. And if He is with me in all situations and circumstances, all will be well. But He does expect me to: "Go now and leave my life of sin."

If you are going through an impossible situation where you see no positive solution, step outside of your emotions and begin to praise Him. Spend all your time in His presence, praising Him, and asking for the grace needed for whatever He wills for your situation.

Most often we waste so much time trying to convince God how to do things. But God is not really concerned about everything going our way. He is working all things out for the good to those of us who love Him.

God My Healer

At this point, Yeshua had saved me, He had delivered me from drugs, and He had comforted my children and me. Now I was about to know Him as my healer.

I started spending more time with the Lord by myself. At night before I put my children to bed I would read them Scriptures and have a time of prayer with them. I would go into my bedroom and spend time by myself sitting in the presence of the Lord. Psalm 46:10 says, *"Be still, and know that I am God; I will be exalted among the nations, I will be exalted in the earth."*

I remember the first time I was trying to be still before the Lord, my mind kept wandering and I would lose concentration on the Lord. I would begin to either think about bills, food, or other fears I still had. A lot of us give up waiting on the Lord because it's difficult to train the mind to fall in line with the word of God. It is so important in our walk that we develop a time of waiting on the Lord. We all make so many mistakes regarding decisions for our lives because we lack the ability to wait. *Psalm 139:23 says, "Search me, God, and know my heart; test me and know my anxious thoughts."* God was now going to test me so I could learn to overcome anything in my life that caused anxiety.

As I sat on the floor beside my bed, I began to praise Him and tell Him what an awesome God He is. I thanked Him for saving me and I began to pray differently. My prayer began something like this: "Lord, here I am, show me how I can serve You better." It felt as if I had been sitting on my floor for a long time when suddenly I got what I'd call a flash back or a vision. I was taken back to my childhood, and saw different memories that were especially painful to me. I saw myself hiding because I was embarrassed to be seen without shoes and wearing torn cloths. The other children would constantly make fun of me. This was part of the growing pains that contributed to my insecurities.

One of my worst hurts was the rejection from my father. If you grow up without a father's love and approval, you will go through life with a void, looking for someone to fill it. I saw a vision of myself as a child, watching my dad from the corner of our two-room home with tears in my eyes. He wouldn't let me get near him because he would say I wasn't his child. When I would ask my mother about it, she would always deny it. She always said my dad was crazy. So I grew up very confused about the relationship between my father and me. I used to wonder why he didn't love me. What was wrong with me? This is another reason why I tried so hard to find someone to love me. I grew up with that void in my life.

I also watched myself as my mother forced me into going to the grocery store. I hated going because there were many times I didn't have shoes, and I would burn my feet during the summer. I also had to pull out stickers from my feet. It was always a painful ordeal to go to the store. I had to run from tree to tree seeking shade for my burning feet. I would have to steal food just so I could eat. There were many times in my childhood when I didn't have anything to eat, so I would go to the stores and steal. I was always so scared, but I was always so hungry.

When I started high school, some of the teachers were very prejudiced and cruel. Several teachers would laugh at me and make terrible comments. I remembered one teacher who embarrassed me in front of the whole class. I was tired from walking to school one day and began to slouch in my chair. My teacher corrected me by saying, "You stupid little Mexican. You'll never amount to anything. You can't even sit correctly!"

I was so embarrassed, and as soon as the class was finished, I went to the bathroom and cried. These are only some of the experiences I went through in my formative years. I had all this anger bottled up in me and didn't know how to get rid of it. I have had to learn that God must heal us from the inside; only then can our broken hearts be made new.

As I saw and remembered all these things, I began to cry. It was as though the Lord was saying: "I need to take you back in order to heal your broken heart." There was a strong presence of the Lord that night. For the first time in my life, I felt the arms of a loving father holding me.

You have to understand that the father I grew up with, and whom I loved, was not my biological father. While my "father" was stationed in Germany during World War II, my mother met my biological father and dated him for the length of time her husband was away. She got pregnant by him and I was born. This was the reason my dad couldn't love me back. I was not aware of the fact my dad was not my biological father. Therefore the rejection was very hurtful and confusing. I would often go behind an adobe wall by the house and cry, always wondering what was wrong with me. Why didn't my dad love me? I grew up before that question was answered.

I remember one time when my mom insisted my dad take me with him to visit his mother. When we got to her house she would not allow me to go inside. I had to wait outside until my dad was ready to go home. For hours, I had to sit under a tree outside their house because his family did not want me around. I grew up with so many other hurts and very confused.

There were 10 in our family at that time and we lived in a two-room house. At night my mother would put a blanket on the floor and that's where we slept. I used to go to school with torn shoes, wearing the same clothes all the time. I put newspaper, or any kind of paper, into the soles of my shoes so the nails from the shoes would not hurt my feet. The father I grew up with was an alcoholic therefore we never had any money to do anything. During my teen years I began feeling a lot of anger towards my mother, and hatred towards my dad. I remember every time I would ask for something, they were never able to provide it. My dad and I never talked so I was unable ask him for anything. Also growing up in a Barrio, one goes through their childhood fighting their way in and out of situations. Most people who grow up in a Barrio wind up being drug addicts. It's a kind of life people give up on. I was always a very determined person and I promised myself I was not going to continue living in poverty. I was determined to make something of myself no matter what I had to do!

It's important that we understand where our fears, insecurities and everything else that shaped our lives, originated. This way, we don't keep blaming the wrong people. This is why a lot of marriages and other relationships fail. People grow up with all these wounds and get married for the wrong reasons. We eventually get divorced because we can't get along with our spouse or because we blame each other for not understanding the other's needs. If we don't take the time to get healed we will continue making the same mistakes. Only Yeshua's work of the Holy Spirit in us can change our hearts.

First He shows us our hurts, and then He gives us the opportunity to forgive the person or persons who hurt us. And after we forgive He is able to heal and restore our hearts.

> *"No one sews a patch of unshrunk cloth on an old garment, for the patch will pull away from the garment, making the tear worse. Neither do people pour new wine into old wineskins. If they do, the skins will burst; the wine will run out and the wineskins will be ruined. No, they pour new wine into new wineskins, and both are preserved."* [Matthew 9:16-17]

A major cause for the lack of maturity in the Lord's body today is people come into a born-again experience and continue to live their lives as before. We have to allow God, through his Holy Spirit, to cleanse our bodies from all our impurities so He can become greater in us. As I continued sitting in the presence of the Lord, He would show me things and then heal my broken heart as I forgave.

The reason I am sharing some of my childhood is because I grew up with all these disappointments, rejections and ridicules. Living in a Barrio makes one tough and it had hardened me. It was very hard for me in that environment because I did not want to get involved with gangs. I was determined to get out of there no matter what it took. The older I got the angrier I became. I'm a very strong-willed person, and I promised myself I would make it in life without getting help.

Growing up, there were times when I needed to talk to my mother but she was always too busy. Taking care of all the children and keeping house was a 24-hour a day job for her. I know now she did the best she could with what she had. I loved my mother very much, but I realized I carried a lot of anger towards her. I was angry because she kept on having babies and the financial situation kept getting worse. At the age of about

12, I stopped trying to talk to my dad altogether. I remember always thinking I would never be able to find someone who would be attracted to me. Anything that stems from your upbringing also molds you into the person you are today.

When I met my ex-husband I thought he was the greatest thing that ever happened to me. My insecurities and rejections caused me to feel that if someone fell in love with me or gave me any type of attention, he would be doing me a favor and I would be indebted to him for the rest of my life.

My ex-husband was very popular at school and I felt very lucky that he even took the time to talk to me, much less ask for a date. At 16, I ran away from home just to hurt my mother. That night I got pregnant. The father of my child was 18-years old. We got married due to pressures from both of our families. He never really wanted to get married or have a baby.

Looking back now, I can understand that; we were both just kids. Even though I knew the father of our baby didn't really want to get married, I went ahead and married him at our parents' request. And quite honestly, I saw it as a way out of my home. A lot of times people think if you run from a situation, things will improve. We may change one person for another but the problems remain the same. We are the same person with the same problems and pains. Only Yeshua can change us, and only if we change will our lives get better.

It was important that the Lord took me back to my childhood experiences in order to get completely healed from my past; otherwise I would be starting a new life with old baggage. And so before God could begin to pour of Himself into me, He had a lot of work to do in me.

> *Don't you know that you yourselves are God's temple and that God's Spirit dwells in your midst? If anyone destroys God's temple, God will destroy that person; for God's temple is sacred, and you together are that temple.* [1 Corinthians 3:16-17]

As the Lord continued healing my broken heart, He started transforming it to a heart of flesh. I can only describe what was taking place in me as a butterfly struggling to come out of a cocoon. When I was born, I was an innocent baby, but since my mother didn't know the Lord, I was formed by the world and all its ugliness. By the time I came to know the Lord, the person that God wanted me to be, was nowhere to be found. Who was I under all that hurt, rejection and disappointment? God was forming me into the person He had intended me to become. If one doesn't deal with all these things they will continue to make the same mistakes. They will be walking the Christian walk with the same wounded heart. Every time the Lord healed me of a certain wound or rejection or disappointment, I felt like I had just shed another skin, somewhat like a snake.

There can also be a danger in going back to the past because if you don't understand the reason the Lord does this, you can get caught up in self pity or blaming whoever hurt you. Therefore, this can become a reason or an excuse for your failure to grow in the Lord. We have to remember that we have a Healer that is far bigger than all our wounds put together.

After the Lord brought me through my childhood healing, He began teaching me how to forgive. There were many people I hated and held anger towards.

At this particular time, I hated my ex-husband and my boss at work the most. It was very hard for me to forgive my ex-husband for what he had done and for what he had put us through. I hated him with a passion, even as a believer I couldn't find it in myself to forgive him for all his cutting remarks and never-satisfied attitude. When I first got saved, my prayer for these two people went like this: "Lord Yeshua, please let me know how I can help assure these two people burn in hell." Several nights I prayed like this. Also, I would pray for the Lord to show me how we (the Lord and I) could make my ex-husband pay for what he had done. Understand I used to blame my ex-husband for the total destruction of my life. It was his fault, I thought.

I prayed the same prayer for several nights. I was sitting in the presence of the Lord this one night, still waiting for an answer, when I heard His voice say, "Love him." When I heard it, I automatically rebuked the thought and commanded Satan to get away from me. I thought to myself: "There's no way God is going to forgive these two individuals. They need to go to hell!" Again I prayed, and this time I heard the Lord's quiet response to my prayer. He said, "Love them." I was reminded of a verse in the New Covenant:

> *"You have heard that it was said, 'Love your neighbor and hate your enemy.' But I tell you, love your enemies and pray for those who persecute you, that you may be children of your Father in heaven. He causes his sun to rise on the evil and the good, and sends rain on the righteous and the unrighteous."* [Matthew 5:43-45]

I began to cry because I felt these two particular people didn't deserve to go to heaven. It's hard to find good teaching in the area of forgiveness. People seek revenge, and I wanted the people who hurt my boys and me to be punished. I had to learn I was being conformed to the image of my Messiah, and He was teaching me who He was, and how He viewed the ones who don't know Him in this world.

The first person the Lord taught me how to love and forgive was my boss. After a couple of weeks of praying and crying, I was finally at a place to say to the Lord, "Okay, please give me the grace I need in order to do this." In learning to forgive, I would remember the Scripture where Yeshua tells us to love our enemies and bless those who curse you. I remember thinking about how I was sure the Lord knew I did not want to forgive these people, but I did want to do what would make my Lord happy. I wanted to obey Him in everything.

I know I walk by faith, and in faith I pray for my enemies and trust Yeshua will put the love only He can give in my heart. I made the decision to yield my heart to Yeshua so He would be able to express His love through me. I asked the Lord what He wanted me to do.

My boss had a plant in his office that needed watering, and he used to drink Coke and take aspirin all day long. The Lord led me to water his plant, and if that wasn't humiliating enough I had to buy him a Coke now and then. I remember the first time I went into his office to water his plant. He was shocked! He turned around and asked me, "What the blank are you doing?" I told him Yeshua had told me to water his plant. He told me to hurry up and get out of there. I finished watering the plant and then went to the bathroom and cried. What I was doing was so contrary to what I wanted to do. I was learning to die to self so others might live.

I did not want to do nice things for this man. As time went on, what the Lord had asked me to do, got easier. When we do things, whatever it is, as unto the Lord, we can overcome all obstacles through Him. Remember, it is the Spirit living in us that is doing the loving as we continue to yield our lives to His will.

Treating my boss this way went on for about 1½ years before any type of positive response manifested from him. One day, he called me into his office and asked me to close the door. Then he asked what caused me to change so much. And there it was—the reason for my serving him. That day, I was able to share the Lord with him and let him know Yeshua loved him. My boss and his family are now saved and attend a Spirit-filled Church.

After I saw what the Lord did with my boss, I began to better understand why I had to become a servant for Him. The Lord was showing me that my life now had nothing to do with the affairs of the world, but it had to do with the salvation of people. Even though I had gone through this forgiveness process with my boss, when it was time to forgive my ex-husband, it was a far more difficult process.

> *"But I tell you, love your enemies and pray for those who persecute you, that you may be children of your Father in heaven."* [Matthew 5:44]

The reason this was harder was because my sons were so affected by what he did or didn't do to them and for them. There are Scriptures we have a tendency to confess with our mouth but they never become part of our lives. In tears, I prayed to the Lord and told him I was going to start praying blessings for my ex-husband, in faith and obedience.

> *Now faith is confidence in what we hope for and assurance about what we do not see.* [Hebrews 11:1]

Faith begins with the spoken Word of God, in obedience. Next comes believing the Holy Spirit living in us is able to produce the fruit of the Spirit of God, which is, ultimately, to do God's will. I prayed for my ex-husband by confessing God's word and trusted Him to change my heart so, at some point, my prayers would be coming from my heart instead of just my mouth. God is the only one who can unconditionally love our enemies, and as we learn to yield our lives to Him daily, He will be reflected more and more in our lives, and we too will be able to love them.

I had been praying for my ex-husband for several months, though I had not seen or heard from him in years. One Saturday afternoon, my ex-husband called and asked if he could see the boys. I took his number and told him I would call him back. I had not heard from him for years, and suddenly he calls and calmly asks to visit. I was so angry when I hung up the phone that I went to my bedroom and began to cry. I had no idea what was the right thing to do, so I asked the Lord for His guidance. I thought of my boys, who were playing at the park across the street. I asked the Lord, "What do you want me to do? What do I say to him?" I heard the Lord tell me to ask my ex-husband to forgive me. I got very upset at the Lord for a moment. I kept wondering why the Lord would tell me to ask my ex-husband to forgive me. The idea seemed ridiculous. I wasn't the one who cheated! I wasn't the one who didn't pay child support! I kept thinking if I asked him for forgiveness he was going to continue laughing at me and begin to think I was the same weak woman he knew back when we divorced.

As I sat quietly before the Lord trying to make sense of what I heard Him say to me, I began to understand what God was doing. I had my first child two months before my 17th birthday. So, there were many areas where I had failed my husband in our marriage. I had inhibitions about sex, and insecurities about my body. I was a child and acted as such in many ways. I didn't know much about most things in life, yet I had wanted my ex-husband to fulfill my every desire. The love I had for him was the kind of love that is fantasized. It was make-believe. Neither one of us were ready for marriage when we took our vows.

The reason God told me to ask for forgiveness from him was so I would take note of the areas where I had failed him. God was not asking me to assume the entire fault for our divorce, but certainly until the Lord put me through this process, I had never examined my shortcomings in our marriage. I failed my ex-husband in many areas, more than likely due to my age, fears and insecurities from my formative years. Lots of divorced people need to take responsibility for areas where they failed one another. Two people make vows in a marriage. And it also takes two people to fail each other. It is important that we seek the Lord, and ask Him to show us the areas we have failed, and the mistakes we have made in our lives and relationships. If we do not correct these areas, we will not be able to succeed in future relationships and situations. It is natural to always blame the other person rather than to ask the Lord to show us where we need to change. I called my ex-husband back and told him he could come over and see the boys.

When he arrived, my heart was racing. I hadn't seen him for at least two years. I invited him in and offered him something to drink. He was looking at me as if I was some strange person. Since we divorced, I had nothing but hate for him. Never would I have thought of having him come over to see the boys nor offer him a glass of tea. Before he said too much, I told him I had something to say to him. He thought I was going to blast him again for the past. I told him I was a Christian now and Yeshua had healed my heart from our divorce. I asked him to forgive me for the areas where I had failed him in our marriage. I also told him I forgave him for what he had done. He stared at me, completely speechless, for a few minutes. Needless to say, he didn't know what to make of my changed attitude. After we were done talking, he spent the rest of the afternoon with the boys.

From the moment he left, I felt like a brand new person. God had totally healed my heart from the hurt of divorce. He continued to neglect responsibility, and still wouldn't pay child support, but none of that mattered I was totally set free. To this day I don't feel anger, or any kind of ill feelings towards him. After I asked for forgiveness, I was healed and was able to see my ex-husband as a lost child of God, as I once was. God loves us all and wants us to know Him.

My ex-husband now lives in El Paso, Texas with his wife and he has developed a relationship with my sons. My Lord continues His work of healing in all of them. In December 2008, I had the privilege of leading my ex-husband and his wife to the Lord. I also had the privilege of leading all of my ex-husband's family to the Lord. Praises be to His Mighty Name! Oh, what God can do if we dare to become fools for the name of Yeshua.

As the Lord continued to show me areas of my life, I was quick to acknowledge the hurt, anger and unforgiveness. I learned to let him have whatever area he wanted to heal. Now I could afford to forgive because Yeshua was starting to give me a heart of flesh. I learned that Yeshua loves those who had hurt me. Once you understand God's love for the lost, you realize the people who hurt you are just as hurt as you are. Until you are willing to do this, you will continue walking with a heart of stone.

There were lots of people who had hurt me, and in turn, I had hurt them. I prayed to the Lord and asked Him to show me what I could do to make things right. There were quite a few people I had really hurt. I wrote down the names of these people, went to the bank and took out all the money I had, which was about $1,000. I went and bought Bibles and took them to each person with a written note inside the Bible asking them for forgiveness and letting them know Yeshua loves them.

My healing continues to this day. The more time I spend with the Lord, the better person I become. One thing I need to remember is that the person who lives in the flesh will never change. It is only by yielding to him that I begin to die to myself and He begins to live through me. There is no one good except the Lord. If I begin to think I am a good person now, I deceive myself and maybe begin to get pious attitude. If I don't spend time with the Lord and continue to let Him fill me with His Spirit daily, I can become the same ugly person I was before Him. We need to remember this so we don't ever get to a place of thinking we don't need His grace for living this life. I began to change the way I prayed. I would take prayer step by step, and be in His presence every night. I would say to Him: "Lord I want to praise you for everything that is taking place in my life right now. I want to love you, no matter the circumstances."

When God sees your utmost desire is to serve Him wholeheartedly, He begins to fill you with the faith you need to deal with whatever circumstance you are in. I would ask Him to fill me with His gentleness so that my gentleness would be evident to all. I would ask Him to be near to me 24 hours a day. I didn't want to be without Him for one second.

I was now about 2½ years old in the Lord and I would still get anxious about certain things. I would immediately confess my anxiety as sin and would cry out for God's mercy to be poured on me to be able to overcome. My anxious thoughts became less and less. I learned to praise him for the awesomeness of who he is. I confessed my sins before him for cleansing, and then I would pray and petition him for all my needs. God is aware of our needs before we ask him for help. For our sake, He uses situations in our lives to train us to become the people of faith we need to become in order to better serve Him and follow him all the days of our lives. I began to thank Him every single day for choosing me as one of his children.

Some time had passed and I was still living at my sister's house. I came to a place where I told the Lord if this is where He wanted me to live, then I wanted to be okay with it. Although I would say to him: "I would prefer a house or an apartment for my boys and myself." I was no longer anxious about the situation. When praying for a house I used to think to myself: "What am I going to use for finances to pay deposits on an apartment or a house? Even if you gave me a house I don't have the money for a deposit or first month's rent. So I quietly walked this through on a daily basis.

One afternoon, my sister got a call from an old boyfriend of hers. He asked her if she knew of anyone who would be able to move into a rental house of his. He said the people had moved out without notice and he didn't want the house to be empty. My sister told him I was looking for a house but I didn't have money for a deposit or the first month's rent. He said to my sister, "Tell Irene she can move into the house this weekend, and not to worry about the deposit or the first two months of rent." He said he just wanted someone to move in right away to take care of the house. This was the first of many miracles the Lord preformed for me. Immediately I went to the garage where I was staying, got on my knees and thanked the Lord for what He had done for me.

We moved into the house the following weekend. It was a three bedroom, two bath house. The thing I needed to learn is that when I was ready to give up my Isaac's and put them on the altar of God, He releases the answer to our prayers. God doesn't always say yes to my wants. But He always provides my needs. I learned to pray and ask Him to put His desires in my heart so that I would be sure I was praying for His will in my life. He promises never to leave us nor forsake us. We can trust Him, because He loves us so much. Still, the trials continued.

Irene and Brother Carlos

Irene and Sisters Back Yard

Irene and Siblings Front Yard

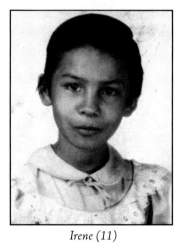
Irene (11)

Irene and Siblings at Grandma's Home

Irene's 15th Birthday

Irene, Husband Alex, and Sister Mary and Friend

Irene (27), Sons Michael and Paul

Irene (28)

Irene (28)

Irene (28) on Drugs

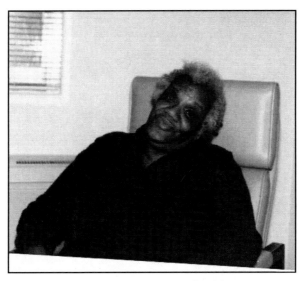
Mama Luke, My Spiritual Mother

Irene Engaged to Yossi

Irene and Yossi's Wedding 1985

Alex, Tovah, Michael, and Paul

Joshua

Irene, Yossi, and Joshua in Israel

Irene and Tovah

14

Marriage in a Worldly Way

One week after we were in our own house I got very sick during the night and my son Woody (Alex) had to take me to the emergency room. The doctors told me they had to remove my gallbladder immediately. The following morning, I had surgery. The doctor assured me it was a very common operation and I would be back on my feet within a couple of weeks. As it turned out, there were complications. I went to the hospital the first week in January and I wasn't able to return to work until the end of April. I was so sick for all those months there were times I thought I was going to die.

I couldn't keep any food in my stomach for any length of time. As soon as I would eat, I would throw up. I weighed a whole 98 pounds. My mother came and stayed with me and took care of the boys. All the while I was sick; I kept hanging on and confessing God's Word. Thank God for the job I had at the time. I was able to go on medical leave and was receiving my full pay check for the time I was gone.

I can do all this through Him Who gives me strength. [Philippians 4:13]

Up to this point in my life I had never been sick. The Lord used the situation to teach me patience and dependency on him. I know a lot of people think that believers in Yeshua should not get sick, but I'm here to tell you that trials and sicknesses for believers are very scriptural. God doesn't make us sick, but He allows and uses everything in our lives to teach us because He loves us. The Bible has much to say about sickness and suffering for Yeshua's sake.

> *I consider that our present sufferings are not worth comparing with the glory that will be revealed in us.* [Romans 8:18]

> *In the same way, the Spirit helps us in our weakness. We do not know what we ought to pray for, but the Spirit Himself intercedes for us through wordless groans. And He who searches our hearts knows the mind of the Spirit, because the Spirit intercedes for God's people in accordance with the will of God.* [Romans 8:26-27]

As a single parent, the last thing I needed was to get sick. I felt bad because my mother had to come and take care of me. She had so much responsibility at her own home. That is one thing I admired about my mother, she never gave up, regardless of the circumstances. The time my mother and I spent together while I was sick allowed us the time to talk about things that otherwise would've been left unsaid. It brought healing to both of us. My mother was a very good woman and her example of courage was what I learned to admire and follow.

During my stay in the hospital, the doctor who attended me was a handsome man who had lost his wife to an illness. He was attracted to me and would come visit me at home. I began to ask the Lord if this man was sent from Him. At first I was confused because this doctor started coming to the house and talking about marriage. He would bring me pictures of his ranch and would tell me how happy my boys would be living at a place like this. At the same time, Don heard I was sick and started coming over to bring groceries. My mother was not a believer at the time, and so she would accept groceries and money from Don. She couldn't understand my life with the Lord yet. She thought I was crazy for leaving such a financially secure relationship. After much prayer and asking the Lord about these men, He answered me by showing me these Scriptures:

> *Do not be yoked together with unbelievers. For what do righteousness and wickedness have in common? Or what fellowship can light*

have with darkness? What harmony is there between Messiah and Belial? Or what does a believer have in common with an unbeliever? [2 Corinthians 6:14-15]

And these two men were unbelievers. Sometimes we try to justify or rationalize a relationship because we really want what we see in front of us. God will never send you an unbeliever to marry. God will never go against His word. I knew neither of these two men was sent from God, so I asked them both not to come over anymore. The Lord then comforted me with more Scripture.

"For your Maker is your husband— the Lord Almighty is His Name— the Holy One of Israel is your Redeemer; He is called the God of all the earth." [Isaiah 54:5]

The Lord was saying to me, from this day forward He was my husband and I was to depend on no one else except Him. I remember telling the Lord I was tired of having so much responsibility and not knowing how to raise my boys. I had made so many mistakes. Now it looked like I was about to start from square one again. The Lord answered me with Scripture once again:

"All your children will be taught by the Lord, and great will be their peace. In righteousness you will be established: Tyranny will be far from you; you will have nothing to fear. Terror will be far removed; it will not come near you." [Isaiah 54:13-14]

After the Lord gave me the Scriptures about Him being my husband and how He was going to teach my boys Himself, I confessed to the Lord I was still scared but I was going to trust Him. I felt a heavy burden being lifted off me once I decided to accept all He had told me.

A couple of weeks went by and the more I thought of the reasons why I had entertained the idea of marriage, the more I realized I didn't want to get married again. I had thought of a man helping me with finances and other areas that were hard for me. These are not the reasons I or anyone else should look to get married. At the time I first got saved, I attended many Bible studies, but I didn't remember hearing any teachings on marriage for a believer. We see in Scripture every marriage that took place was for a continuation of God's plan for the redemption of the world. We see examples like Abraham and Sarah, Isaac and Rebecca, Boaz and Ruth and many more. These examples show God orchestrating marriages in order to accomplish His purpose. As believers, we need to have the same thought pattern concerning marriage. After reading this, some may say that I'm being too fanatical on the issue of marriage.

Let me ask a question at this point: If marriage is the solution to our problems, why are there so many divorces? The divorce rate among believers is almost as high as it is in the world. Shouldn't we, as the body of Messiah, be the example of what a marriage ought to be? Take a moment and think about it.

For we are God's handiwork, created in Messiah Yeshua to do good works, which God prepared in advance for us to do. [Ephesians 2:10]

Marriages in the body of Messiah as a whole are in trouble today because we have worldly thoughts regarding marriage. I believe the reason the divorce rate in the body of the Messiah is so high is because there is lack of understanding of the fact that our lives do not belong to us.

I have been crucified with Messiah and I no longer live, but Messiah lives in me. The life I now live in the body, I live by faith in the Son of God, Who loved me and gave Himself for me. [Galatians 2:20]

There has to be a difference in the way we approach life once we've being enlightened by our salvation through God's word and through His Holy Spirit. Because I lived so many years in a worldly life style, I was able to see the similarities of world standards in the Church. Again, I don't want to come across as judging anyone, but on the other hand, I pray we as the people of God are willing to be a separate people and look to do His will in all matters. Marriage is such a special union made in heaven, by God, for His delight. That is why Satan works so hard to destroy it. Once the marriage is destroyed, his target becomes our children. If Yeshua is not the answer, what do we say to our children when they ask: "If Yeshua couldn't save this marriage, what chance do I have?"

When I found Yeshua, He had to be the total answer for me and for my children. I can't think of what else I could have told them, or to where, or to whom, to point them to for an answer.

When I was in the world, it was very seldom I didn't have a date. When I started attending church services, men began asking me for dates. I prayed and asked the Lord if it was OK with Him if I went out. I figured it would be OK, but God emphatically said, "No!"

So I began to question the Lord about going out on what I deemed as an innocent dinner date. I even did a study on dating—but I found little to nothing on the matter. As I sat in God's presence—trying to understand— He began to teach me. First of all, one of the reasons I wanted to go out on a date was because I was lonely. The second reason flirts with deception. I used to think that if a man asked me out on a date, he was looking for someone to start a long lasting relationship with. Again, I found myself trying to justify me going on dates. I already knew God said "NO" to dating. I finally made the decision not to date.

Sometime later, one of the Elders of the church came to me and wanted me to meet a friend of his. He said this man was a godly man and that he would be a good companion for me and that this man would be a good father to my boys. I shared with him my conviction on dating. He went on to say that God wanted me to be happy. I finally agreed as a favor to my elder friend to go out on a date with this man.

I justified the situation by thinking maybe God hadn't said, "No," it was just my imagination or something like that. After all, this time an elder of the church set me up with this man. Being an elder, I thought, he must certainly hear from God. So I went on the date. The man was well known in the church, he had a good reputation (or so it seemed) and came recommended, so I was sure he was a "godly man"—whatever that meant.

I hear lots of women use the term, godly man, when praying for a husband. A godly man is one who loves God, and does his best to keep relationship with Him and then with his family. But this doesn't mean he is perfect. Both men and women have lots of flaws in their lives to work out with the Lord. Growth in the Lord is ongoing until you see Him face to face.

The man picked me up, took me to dinner at a real nice restaurant and then proceeded to take me to a nightclub for dancing. When he drove into the parking lot of the nightclub, I asked him what was he was doing? He said it was a surprise. He stopped the truck and opened the door for me to get out. Please remember I was only 1 1/2-yrs. old in the Lord. This man supposedly had been a Christian for many years and was allowed to teach in the church. Needless to say I was shocked. I didn't get out of the truck. I asked him to take me home.

I asked him how he could be a believer in Yeshua and call himself a Christian and then dare to take a date to a nightclub. He answered by saying, "What else is there to do?"

I said to him, "I just came out of the world and left all this behind; I don't want anything to do with clubs or any such things, please take me home."

I was very surprised when he got upset over the issue. While we were driving home, neither of us said a word. When we got to my house, he stopped the truck and apologized to me. We sat in his truck talking for a couple of minutes. He wanted to come in and meet my children. I told him no. At this point I realized my mistake of being disobedient to God.

He then asked if we could try again and maybe the next time would be different. Again I said, "No." I told him I should not have gone out because this was my conviction about dating. He calmed down and asked if he could kiss me good night on the cheek. I just wanted him to leave so I agreed to let him kiss me on the cheek. As he leaned over to kiss me, he grabbed my arm and told me how beautiful he thought I was and that a woman like me shouldn't be alone. I got a bit frightened at this point. I tried to pull away, but the more I tried to pull away the more forceful he became. He then tried to get his hands all over me. By this time I was crying and I started asking the Lord for help.

He suddenly stopped and again apologized for his actions. But he wasn't sorry. He said God understands the sexual desires we have, and being Christians has nothing to do with it. He said Christians have the same needs as everyone else. I started to get out of his car and turned and called him a hypocrite. I told him if he ever came near me or called I would go straight to the pastor and expose him for what he really was. All this happened in a matter of 15 minutes or so. Needless to say, this cured my dating itch.

Another situation came up with another man at the same church (the church had a big attendance), and this man was well known at the church as well. He came up to me on several occasions and asked if I would go out to dinner. I always said, "No thank you, I don't believe in dating." The last time he asked me out I again said, "No, thank you." I tried to be as nice as I could.

He got upset and said, "it's not like I'm asking you to marry me, I'm just asking for a date.

When he said this I turned and asked him, "If you're not looking for a wife, then why date?"

He said, "I don't need a wife, I just get lonely sometimes."

The reason I share these incidents is because there is a lot of dating happening in the body of Messiah today. And what I noticed was that dating in the Lord, was done as carelessly as it is done in the world. The more I was around believers the more I realized there was very little difference in the way a relation was approached. The Bible tells us to respect each other and that men ought to treat women in the Lord as sisters. So why are brothers and sisters in kissing-dating relations? How long can a brother or sister in the Lord continue to stay pure in a relationship? Think about it for a moment. We are human and a people of many weaknesses. It's only by the grace of God that we're able to stay pure in areas having to do with relationships.

> *But among you there must not be even a hint of sexual immorality, or of any kind of impurity, or of greed, because these are improper for God's holy people. Nor should there be obscenity, foolish talk or coarse joking, which are out of place, but rather thanksgiving. For of this you can be sure: No immoral, impure or greedy person—such a person is an idolater—has any inheritance in the kingdom of Messiah and of God. [Ephesians 5:3-5]*

I can tell you of many more incidents I went through with brothers in the Lord. At the time I began to blame men—again—for hurting women and being insensitive. As I grew in the Lord, I realized there was a great need for teaching about dating and marriage.

The Lord convicted me about the way I dressed. Coming from the world, I dressed in a way that was comfortable for the world's eyes. In the Lord, it is our responsibility to dress properly and, in doing this, we learn to respect ourselves as well. Also we help our brothers in areas where some might be struggling with sexual problems. I want to put the responsibility where it ought to be. Everyone is going to be accountable to God one day and I, as a woman, decided from that day I would not be a stumbling block for any of my brothers in the Lord.

I'll share a story that illustrates the seriousness of proper attire: When I came to know the Lord, I was still considered "desirable." I wore a size 3 dress and my jeans were so tight, in reality, I should've been wearing a size 4. As I was leaving service one evening, I approached the door and there was a young man who had just started attending and was not yet saved. As I passed by him he slapped me on my behind! I was so embarrassed. Other people who were there saw what happened and immediately went to leadership and told. The young man was brought into the office. I didn't want to stay because I was embarrassed so I left and got in my car.

While I sat in my car, I was convicted on how I was dressed. My pants were too tight. They looked like they were painted on me. I began to feel responsible for what this young man had done. I went back inside to the office where the leadership was dealing with him and asked to speak. I looked at the young man and asked him to forgive me for wearing my jeans too tight and causing him to stumble. He started crying and asked me to forgive him. He became one of our best friends. If I had not assumed responsibility for the way I looked, it would have made me think it was entirely his fault. Yes, what he did was absolutely wrong, but if I hadn't been dressed this way maybe it wouldn't have happened. We need to be careful not to make our brothers stumble.

I learned to be more careful of how I dressed. The Bible tells us to dress modestly. So, I decided to start dressing appropriately and to be careful not to give wrong impressions to my brothers in the Lord. In other words, I was going to do my best to be a "godly woman," and wait until God, if He so chose, would bring me a husband. And until that day, I would not date! Many may disagree with me on this issue, but in counseling many young sisters in the Lord, I've found there is a lot of hurt and disappointment in relationships that started and ended nowhere. We have to begin to teach on the differences of being a woman and what a date means to a woman, and being a man and what a date means to a man. Until we understand each other and the way God made us, then and only then, will we be ready to respect each other and understand why God says to treat each other like brothers and sisters.

God My Provider

As I continued with the Lord there were times when I didn't know what I was going to feed my boys for dinner. I would go to a nearby park during my lunch hour at work and begin to talk to the Lord. I would tell Him, "You know my situation concerning finances and food. I don't have any food at home to feed my boys, but I thank You for taking care of this already."

While I was praying, my mind was saying, "Yeah, sure. How is He really going to do this?" But regardless of what I was thinking, I was still confessing the word of God.

Now faith is confidence in what we hope for and assurance about what we do not see. [Hebrews 11:1]

This particular day my prayer was answered by the time I got back from lunch. My sister called and told me her maid was preparing my favorite food and was bringing it over for the boys and myself for dinner. There was many times the Lord fed us this way. Some might wonder why God would feed us in this manner. As you study Scripture you find many instances where God sends his people to be fed by others. Read *2 Kings 4:8-9* and other examples of how God takes good care of His people.

I'm not saying God is not able to provide in our own home, but looking back He was working out His character in me. I had become very self-sufficient and I was never asking anyone for anything. God had to teach me humility, and at the same time, He was teaching me to trust Him. Another time my children and I were praying and my son Michael wanted to pray and ask Yeshua to send us some steaks. We hadn't eaten steak in a long time. I than asked him to pray. I didn't have the faith to believe God for steak. I'm sure Yeshua will answer your prayer, I told him." The reason I asked him to pray was because I didn't believe that the Lord was interested in sending us steaks. After I put them to bed, I had to go and apologize to the Lord for my lack of faith in this area. I said to the Lord, I don't know how you would do this, but for the sake of my Michael's faith, please send him some steak."

The following morning began as any other morning, getting the boys ready for school, giving them breakfast, and rushing out to drop them off at school and getting to work by 8:00AM. On my way home from work that afternoon, I stopped at the store to buy a bag of potatoes and some eggs. When I got home, I began to peel the potatoes we were having for dinner. I was standing over the sink when I heard the front door open. At first I thought it was one of the kids, as I turned around I was surprised to see Don in the kitchen. He had this box and laid it on the kitchen table. I didn't even have time to say more than two words to him. He just said, "I don't know how I did this, but I ordered one box too many for the restaurant and I needed to get rid of these. If you don't want them, just throw them out. The only reason I brought them over was because I thought of the Pest (Michael's nickname) and I decided to bring them over."

He immediately turned around and left. I went and opened the box; it contained 32 filet mignon steaks. I began to cry, as I was seeing the Lord's caring and loving answered prayer for my son. Needless to say, we had a feast that night!

There was a time when Michael needed a jacket. I was still living from paycheck to paycheck and before I got my check it was already spent (maybe some of you can identify with this). I didn't have money to buy my son a jacket. The one he was wearing was too small for him. After prayer that night, he asked me to please buy him a jacket. I told him I had to wait until I got some extra money. After I put him to bed that night, I prayed to the Lord. I said, "Lord, You promised to be my Husband and the Father to my children, please send me a jacket for Michael." It had not been too long since the miracle of the steaks and this was another opportunity for my faith to grow. Again I only saw impossibility. Every time I prayed for something, I always tried to figure out how God would do this or if He would.

> *"For My thoughts are not your thoughts, neither are your ways My ways," declares the Lord. "As the heavens are higher than the earth, so are My ways higher than your ways and My thoughts than your thoughts."* [Isaiah 55:8]

The beauty of learning how to live by faith is that our fears begin to diminish. The needs I had offered to the Lord allowed me to see God at work and it showed me how to trust and to let me know He would always be there for me. Every time I tried to figure out how God was going to answer my prayer, He always answered a totally different way. God doesn't want us to try to figure Him out. We are a people of habit. We tend to form habits and then get comfortable in them. The Lord wants us to always need Him. As long as we have a need, He can work out a miracle. As long as we keep running to our parents, government or other institutions for help, we will not see the miracles of God in our lives. We have to come to a place in our walk with this Mighty God where we believe He is the same God who opened the Red Sea, gave manna from the sky, and water from the rock. The Bible tells us He is the same God yesterday, today and forever. He changes not.

The following week, I took Paul and Michael to the dentist for their check up. I was at the dentist office by 7:30AM. My dentist lived close to the house and he knew I was a single parent. He was always kind enough to see me early so I could get the boys to school and myself to work on time. We got done at the dentist and the boys and I started walking to the car. I was about to get in the car when I noticed a jacket on the back bumper. I went and picked it up and started looking around. I thought maybe someone had being playing there and had forgotten their jacket. It was early in the morning and no one was around. I went back into the building and asked the nurse if the jacket belonged to anyone she knew. She said "no."As I started walking back to the car, the Lord spoke to me and asked, "didn't Michael need a jacket?" I began to take a good look at the jacket. It was brand new and it was exactly Michael's size. I tried the jacket on Michael and it was a perfect fit. I always bought jackets a size bigger to last for at least two winters.

Many times when we pray for something we act like Rhoda in the book of Acts.

> Peter knocked at the outer entrance and a servant named Rhoda came to answer the door. When she recognized Peter's voice, she was so overjoyed she ran back without opening it and exclaimed, "Peter is at the door!" "You're out of your mind," they told her. When she kept insisting that it was so, they said, "It must be his angel." [Acts 12:13-15]

These people had been praying for Peter's release without really believing God was actually going to do it. That is how I felt after I heard Michael say to me from inside the car, "Mom, Yeshua gave me my jacket." Michael put the jacket on and went to school full of joy at what the Lord had done. I went on to work praising and thanking God.

A couple of months passed when there came another opportunity for another miracle. I got behind paying my gas bill and I received a disconnect notice. I was unable to come up with the money I needed. I got home from work to find my gas cut off. I was feeling down and depressed and I kept thinking of what I was going to tell my boys. As it was they would sometimes complain because all we had to eat were eggs, potatoes and rice, and now that the gas had been turned off, I wasn't going to be able to cook at all. I turned and looked up and asked the Lord: "How can You possibly be glorified through this?"

I had a couple of dollars in my wallet and I thought I'd go the store and buy lunch meat for sandwiches. Before I left for the store, I went into the kitchen to wash a couple of frying pans I had left in the sink that morning. When I got done with the dishes, I begin to clean the top of the stove. I started checking the burners to make sure all of them were set on the off button. When I got to the left front burner I turned the knob on and then off again, as I had done with the other three. The burner lit up as I turned it. I immediately turned it off again. I thought nothing of it. I just thought there were fumes in that one burner and that's why it lit up. I tried it again and again and it lit every time. I went outside to check my gas meter and it did have the wire lock on it. I ran back inside and tried the burner again and it lit. There was no gas coming out of the burner, but the burner lit for almost two months until I had enough money to pay the bill. Not only was I able to cook for my family, but we never took a cold shower. Can you imagine this taking place now in this century? How big is your God?

I called Mama Luke (my spiritual mother) and others to come see the miracle the Lord was doing for me. There were so many more miracles God did for my children and me. These are just a few to encourage you to go on and trust the Lord in whatever situation. He will not let you down. I want to take this opportunity to caution you about miracles and visions the Lord may do and show you. The miracles God does for his children are because He is faithful and will always take care of His children. I believe in absolute miracles, or as people say "unexplainable happenings."

I believe, without a doubt, God gives His people visions. Scripture tells us that God's people perish for lack of knowledge or vision. Even though I believe in the miraculous, these provisions God makes for us have absolutely nothing to do with our salvation and obedience to God. Some people make the mistake of thinking because they see things (spiritual as they say) this makes them closer to God or they no longer have to be obedient to God according to Scripture. God does speak to his people, but everything the Spirit of God tells us has to line up with the Word of God. So many people today are going after what some spirit is telling them and are falling into deception by not checking and following the Word of God.

It was December in El Paso, Texas. El Paso does not get much snow, but it does get very cold in the winter. It was a Sunday afternoon and the boys and I were at Mama Luke's house for fellowship time. Someone walked into her house about 8:30PM and commented that a blizzard was headed to El Paso. We turned on the television to confirm and realized it had already started snowing on the west side of town, which is where I lived. I immediately got the boys and myself in the car and started for home. I was praying I would make it home before the storm. El Paso is a city not prepared to handle snow, and the west side of town is rather hilly.

I exited the interstate and proceeded on to the main street heading towards my apartment, but by the time we arrived in the area the blizzard was in full force. I tried to turn onto my street, which was on a hill, but the car kept sliding back. I noticed cars stranded on the side of the road and people walking to their destinations. We were still far from the apartment and we were not dressed for walking in blizzard conditions.

I was stuck in the middle of the road and unable to move and park the car on the side of the road. We were stuck in a non-residential desert area and couldn't call anyone for help. Cell phones were not in existence yet. We had been stranded now for about 1½ hours. I began to get scared. The snow was so thick I couldn't see out my windows. I was afraid the car was not visible to oncoming traffic. The boys and I started praying and we asked Yeshua to come help us. We sat in the car a while longer when all of a sudden there was a knock on my window. I lowered my window and two young men wearing ski masks were standing there. One asked if we needed help. I said, "Yes." He instructed me to stay in the car. He said he and his friend would take care of us. I began to thank the Lord for sending these two young men.

As we were sitting in the car, it began to move. Because of the way it was moving I thought we were sliding and were about to crash into something. I still couldn't see out my windows. We suddenly came to a stop and I opened the door to see what had happened. The two men were standing at the back of the car. The car was now parked on the side of the road close to where we lived within walking distance from our apartment. The reason we still had to walk was because there were cars parked on the side of the road so we could not have parked any closer. I walked around and opened the door for the boys and told them to get out of the car. We were all amazed at what took place. As we were standing there getting ready to walk home I turned around looking for the two men to thank them, but they were gone. We looked, but they were nowhere to be found. And there were no footprints in the snow. As mysteriously as they appeared is how mysteriously they disappeared. As I started walking home the Lord reminded me of a Scripture.

> *If you say, "The Lord is my refuge," and you make the Most High your dwelling, no harm will overtake you, no disaster will come near your tent. For He will command His angels concerning you to guard*

you in all your ways; they will lift you up in their hands, so that you will not strike your foot against a stone. [Psalm 91:9-12]

"He will call on Me, and I will answer him; I will be with him in trouble, I will deliver him and honor him." [Psalm 91:15]

Truly, God gave His angels charge over us! And he will do it for you too.

16

GROWING TO MATURITY

As I continued to learn about walking with Yeshua, I learned to pray and fast.

"When you fast, do not look somber as the hypocrites do, for they disfigure their faces to show others they are fasting. Truly I tell you, they have received their reward in full. But when you fast, put oil on your head and wash your face, so that it will not be obvious to others that you are fasting, but only to your Father, Who is unseen; and your Father, Who sees what is done in secret, will reward you." [Matthew 6:16-18]

I was at a singles prayer night. This meant we got together and did nothing but pray. During this time, the lady leading the prayer time asked the entire group to stand up because she felt led by the Lord to pray for husbands and wives for the group. We all got in a circle, held hands and she began to pray. While she was praying I was thinking to myself, I'm not receiving this prayer because I don't want to get married again.

Some time had passed since my dating incident. I had not entertained a thought of dating again, much less marriage. However, when I got home that night, I felt uneasy in my spirit. I stayed up for awhile and started feeling the conviction of the Holy Spirit concerning the prayer for marriage. Again I had made a decision without consulting the Lord. I repented and asked the Lord to forgive me for rejecting the prayer offered in regard to marriage. I began to pray in this way: "At this point of my life I don't want to get married, but I don't want to rebel against anything You have for my life." I asked the Lord to show me if marriage was in his plans for my life. I prayed and fasted concerning this for a whole week.

At the end of the week, I was sitting during my quiet time and the Lord gave me a vision. I saw myself getting married and dancing in the Church. I saw myself having two more children. I also saw myself living in what I thought was Mexico at the time I had the vision; I didn't understand what I had seen. When the vision ended I was overwhelmed. First of all, when I had this vision I was 33 years old and my boys were 17, 12 and 8. The thought of having children again was overwhelming. After trying to analyze the vision I sort of came to a conclusion maybe this was not from the Lord after all. Besides, dancing in a Church? I had never heard of such a thing. And living in Mexico, I wasn't thrilled with the idea. I called my spiritual mother and asked her to pray with me concerning this vision. She advised me to pray and put it on the shelf. She said, "If it is the Lord it will come to pass, and if it's not the Lord, it will go away."

With this advice, I still continued to pray regarding what I had seen. The Lord showed me I still had a lot of healing to go through before I could be married. At this time the Lord began to deal with the fact I was still carrying unforgiveness against my ex-husband. There was no way I could marry until I dealt with this issue. I started praying for him every night, but when I started praying for him I didn't mean it. The Lord had showed me the scripture "love your enemies, bless them that curse you and do good to those who despitefully use you;" When I first got saved, I prayed this for my ex-husband; "Lord please show me how I can help to ensure my ex- husband goes to hell for all the hurt he has caused me and my children". When you are that hurt you are not able to pray for your enemy and mean it. I went to the Lord with this; Lord I love you and want to do all that you ask, therefore I am going to begin to pray for my ex-husband in obedience to you, but you know I don't mean it. The last thing I wanted to do for him was to pray blessings. I begin praying the scripture every night and believed that somehow God would change my heart. It took about two months praying like this until one night I realized I wasn't angry and felt totally different towards my ex-husband. I no longer saw him as my ex-husband. I saw him as a child of God that needed salvation. I understood that God loved him.

I than included him in our group prayers with my children. It's important that single parents begin the process of healing for their children as well as for themselves if they are ever going to have healthy relationships. My children were very blessed and happy to hear me include their father in our prayers. It took awhile before I could really pray for him from my heart. I noticed as I yielded my heart to the Lord concerning my hurt and anger towards this man, I was beginning to feel some sort of love for him again. I could finally tell the Lord to bless him and really mean it. It takes time to heal from so many years of hurt.

Now, I really have to think when I tried to remember why I hated him so much. Praise the Lord for a new heart.

My boys would sometimes ask me if I no longer hated their father. I was happy to be able to say I no longer hated him. I now understood my ex-husband was a product of what his upbringing created. He also needed to find Yeshua and begin a new life. When you say you forgive someone, the Lord will test you on this. Sometimes he sends that person to you to see if you are mature enough to retain your healing or to see if you respond in the flesh and allow hurt and those past feelings to come back. Pass the test so you can go on. Otherwise you will continue to go through the same thing over and over until you pass the test. What an awesome God we serve!

Search me, God, and know my heart; test me and know my anxious thoughts. See if there is any offensive way in me, and lead me in the way everlasting. [Psalm 139:23-24]

It is so important that we, who have failed in relationships time and time again, begin to examine ourselves. I had no identity other than being "attractive." Facing this label was so important for me to begin the healing process concerning men, and to learn who I was as a woman. I had to learn how to love and trust God as my savior, healer, father and provider. At my age most importantly, He was my Husband and the Father of my children. Why is this important? You will never find a man who will be able to meet all your needs, whether it is emotional, physical or spiritual. Once you have made the Lord your all, then and only then, are you able to trust someone else in your life.

The Lord began to teach me about men, how He had created men for specific purposes and women for specific purposes. When a man and a woman come together, both need to be submitted to the guidance of the Lord, otherwise the relationship will never work out. I had to learn men will always disappoint me and let me down at some point, and I will do the same. It doesn't matter how hard we try to do our best, we always fail at some point. The beauty of this is I had learned how to forgive and pray to get better every day. One necessary ongoing aspect of a Christian marriage is both the husband and wife should pursue a "change-me-God" approach instead of trying to blame each other for mis-understandings. The most important thing in a marriage is to be right with each other so your prayers will not be hindered. I was finally able to respect men, not because of what they did or did not do, but based on what God had taught me about them. The most important thing I was learning is God is always working in ME!

Through the Eyes of a Gentile

If there was only one thing I was finding out about this born-again life it's that my life no longer belongs to me.

> *"I have been crucified with Messiah and I no longer live, but Messiah lives in me. The life I now live in the body, I live by faith in the Son of God, Who loved me and gave Himself for me. I do not set aside the grace of God, for if righteousness could be gained through the law, Messiah died for nothing!"* [Galatians 2:20-21]

After all the healing, deliverance and miracles of provisions, I was beginning to understand the decision I had made to follow Yeshua was truly going to cost me my life, whether by life or by death. Meaning, I needed to learn to pray in accordance to God's will for my life and let go of the things I desired if those things didn't line up with what He would call me to do.

> *I keep asking that the God of our Lord Yeshua the Messiah, the glorious Father, may give you the Spirit of wisdom and revelation, so that you may know Him better. I pray that the eyes of your heart may be enlightened in order that you may know the hope to which He has called you, the riches of His glorious inheritance in His holy people, and His incomparably great power for us who believe.* [Ephesians 1:17-19]

That is what all of us are called to do: Find out what God saved us for.

As I continued to study my Bible, I noticed I was being attracted to Jewish-Gentile Scriptures. I wasn't sure what God was trying to show me, but it was like reading my Bible with a new understanding.

For I am not ashamed of the Good News, because it is the power of God that brings salvation to everyone who believes: first to the Jew, then to the Gentile. [Romans 1:16]

"I, the Lord, have called you in righteousness; I will take hold of your hand. I will keep you and will make you to be a covenant for the people and a light for the Gentiles, to open eyes that are blind, to free captives from prison and to release from the dungeon those who sit in darkness." [Isaiah 42:6-7]

I am talking to you Gentiles. Inasmuch as I am the apostle to the Gentiles, I take pride in my ministry in the hope that I may somehow arouse my own people to envy and save some of them. [Romans 11:13-14]

Oh my! What does this mean? The more I continued reading and studying the book of Romans, the more I became confused.

Again I ask: Did they stumble so as to fall beyond recovery? Not at all! Rather, because of their transgression, **salvation has come to the Gentiles to make Israel envious.** [Romans 11:11]

This was a lot for me to try to understand. I got saved at a non-denominational spirit- filled Church. I went to talk to my pastor to ask him what he thought of what was happening to me and all he said was "we were the new Israel" whatever that meant. He wouldn't explain any further. Come to find out, as I understood things better, he taught replacement theology, which means the Gentile Church has replaced Israel in God's plan.

The only person I could turn to for prayer was Mama Luke, my spiritual mother. Even she didn't understand what was happening to me. She respected my walk with the Lord and so agreed to keep me in prayer. As I continued studying the Scriptures I noticed I was drawn to what the scriptures had to say about the Jewish people. What does this mean? How come no one makes mention of them? Who is a Jew?

I was saved by Yeshua and was told He was the Son of God and he died for me. Aside from that awareness of salvation there wasn't much else that was taught about Him. I began to re-read the gospels and it was as though I was reading the Bible with a different understanding. I began to realize that the whole Bible was a Jewish book. I began to feel very uncomfortable and out of place again. The pastor kept saying I was the spiritual Jew and there was no need for the physical Jew. And others I asked had absolutely no idea what I was talking about. Again, for the first time in my life as a believer, I began to feel alone. What happened to me? Where was the assurance I thought I had found in Yeshua?

I got saved in August 1978. In the spring of 1980, Sid Roth aired on the radio in El Paso. As I listened to his story, he said he was a Jew and he had found his Messiah. More and more, I heard about Jews being saved. I would listen to his message every day. Here I was with all this new knowledge and I had no one to share it with. I had no one I could come to for questions and answers. All I had was Yeshua and the love I had for Him and the love He had for me.

As I was learning all this, I didn't know what to do. As I mentioned at the beginning of the book, I was born to a very poor family, in El Paso. I attended school 9½ years, never graduated high school. So here I was in the midst of all this, not knowing what to do with all I was experiencing. All I could do was pray for God's direction for my children and myself. So you can better understand my lack of education, I didn't know there were still Jewish people. I thought they had lived in the times of Yeshua and they had ended with the death of Yeshua.

My first experience with a Jewish person happened as I was being trained by the Church on how to do outreach. I was assigned to a married couple from the Church and we used to go house-to-house introducing the love of Yeshua. I had gone out with them for a couple of months and watched and heard what they did and said. By now, the husband thought I was ready to share. He told me to get ready as we approached the next house.

I rang the doorbell and a man opened the door. I introduced myself and told him we were in the neighborhood telling people about the love of Yeshua and I asked him if I could share about Yeshua.

He grinned and said to me, "Thank you, but I'm Jewish."

I got so excited and I went on to tell him how excited I was to know that he was related to Yeshua. He again grinned and said, "No, you don't understand, I'm Jewish."

And he was right, I didn't understand. I was excited because this was the first time I was telling someone about Yeshua, and that someone **just happened to be Jewish.** So I asked him, "How does it feel to be related to Yeshua?" He again grinned. By this time my coach was tugging at my shirt and apologized to the man for bothering him. As we walked away, I was excited about what had happened, but I was told never to do that again. I was confused by this reaction.

He said to me, "You never share Yeshua with a Jew."

I've never been one to say, "Okay" or "Yes sir" to anyone, especially if I disagree. I guess that's why I always got in trouble growing up. He went on to say to me Jewish people don't believe in Yeshua, and I needed to always remember not to do that again. I reminded him of the two months I had gone out with them on outreach and asked what difference does it make? He went door-to-door and shared Yeshua with the rest of the community and most of them said they didn't want to hear, and he still continued to go back. I told him I didn't think this was different, so I was going to share Yeshua with everyone. What I was learning in the Church was not what I was reading in the Bible! So I decided to go with what the Bible said.

Until I came to know the Lord, I didn't know Jewish people existed. I know some of you might find that hard to believe, but growing up in El Paso on the wrong side of the tracks, I was pretty naïve and un-educated.

But God chose the foolish things of the world to shame the wise; God chose the weak things of the world to shame the strong. God chose the lowly things of this world and the despised things—and the things that are not—to nullify the things that are, so that no one may boast before Him. [1 Corinthians 1:27-29]

Boy, you talk about being a fool. I knew nothing except what the Bible said, and most of that I was learning as I went along. The Bible was the first complete book I ever read. Not to say I didn't study while I attended school for the 9½ years, but back in 1961, we were still learning the three R's in high school. And I even had a problem with that. I never studied history or geography. When I was growing up, school was never an important subject at home. I got home from school every day and had plenty of chores waiting for me. By the time I was done, it was time to go to bed. There was no time for homework or anything else that had to do with school. So here I was sharing the Good News, with the little that I knew about the Bible.

I continued going to Church on Sundays. I had made friends and felt sort of at home there, though I didn't agree with a lot of what was being taught. However, I kept asking about Passover, which is mentioned in the New Covenant. No one knew anything about it. I asked about it in Bible Study class and the answer I got was: "It's something they celebrated in Old Covenant times."

My response to that answer was, "Then why is it mentioned in the New Covenant and why was Yeshua celebrating it?"

I was told we would discuss it later. Later never came. I was amazed at the fact I was an unschooled person reading the Bible and I was made to believe I was reading it all wrong. Why couldn't these teachers see what I saw? My prayer to the Lord was either they were wrong or I was wrong. "Please let me know," I prayed. I wasn't trying to be disrespectful when I asked questions. I just had questions. And no one could answer them.

The Church I attended used to have Christian concerts on Friday evenings. My friend Cheryl and I used to take our kids to the concerts. A friend of ours moved to the Westside of town. She would drive to the Eastside to attend the concerts and for our kids to play together. All three of us were single parents. I had shared with both my friends what I was feeling regarding my studies in the Bible about Jewish people, not knowing what it all meant.

One Friday after the concert, we were sitting outside and my friend starting asking me about what I had found out about the Jews. I told her no one knew what I was talking about and I still didn't understand what was happening to me. I told her I was still listening to Sid Roth sharing his Jewish experience and so on. I told her I was continuing to study, and I guess God would someday let me know why I was seeing the Scriptures in this way. She began to share with me that she found out there were some Jews getting together on the Westside of town and they were Believers in Yeshua. Nothing more was said about the Jews that night. The following Friday, she came to attend the concert. After the concert we begin to talk again. She told me that she had attended a service at the place where the Jews were meeting. She told me that I should go and try it out. She said the services were very different but very good. I told her I had to pray about going and left it at that.

Again, though I was curious about what I knew God was teaching me in the Bible, I was afraid because I didn't understand what was happening to me. I had made friends in the Church and, at this point, I thought I was good with God. The more I continued studying, the more I realized there were two distinct peoples the Scriptures spoken about, the Jew and the Gentile. I realized I was the Gentile. But what did that mean? I got together with Mama Luke and told her all I was going through, and that it was getting stronger, and I didn't know what to do about it. What does God want me to do? And why do Christians say Jews don't need to be saved? I read the book of Romans over and over trying to make some sense of it. "Why Lord? Why does the Church say Jews can't be saved?" Resounding in my heart, these Scriptures kept speaking to me.

> *For I am not ashamed of the Good News, because it is the power of God that brings salvation to everyone who believes: **first to the Jew**, then to the Gentile. For in the Good News the righteousness of God is revealed—a righteousness that is by faith from first to last, just as it is written: "The righteous will live by faith." [Romans 1:16-17]*

As I continued to read I realized Yeshua celebrated Passover, The Feast of Tabernacles, Feast of Dedication (Chanukah) and other mentioned celebrations. I read but couldn't make sense of it. I asked Mama Luke if she would pray and fast with me, as I wanted God to make things clear to me. I was so troubled by this I began to feel sad because of my lack of understanding. I cried to the Lord for days and asked Him to show me what He wanted. I said to Him, "Lord, all these Scriptures are strong in my heart, but I don't know what to do with them. No one understands me. Please let me know what you want me to do with all this or take this away." I fasted and prayed the same way for about a week.

My friend Cheryl and I were at the concert about two weeks after my fast and my friend from the west side of town came to spend the evening with us. As we were talking, she again began to tell me about the Jews meeting on the west side. She said, "Irene, I attended a service again with the Jews. It was so awesome. They dance and the services are so different. You need to go."

For the first time after months of this being mentioned to me, I felt my spirit leap in me. I thought maybe the Lord was beginning to lead me to an answer to prayer. I told her I would pray about it, but again I didn't do anything with it. This time though, I did continue thinking about it. I finally told the Lord if he wanted me to attend this place, he needed to give me the name, address and all the information I needed. I said to the Lord, "I will go only if I know you are sending me, and if you are sending me you need to come down and give me the address. I will not look for it." So I left it at that.

The following week I was at work and one of the cashier's needed a break so I was covering for her. A young man came in to make a payment on his car and began to say, "Praise the Lord. I will be able to pay off my car in a couple of months."

I agreed with him and responded, "This is praise the Lord. Paying your car off is a great accomplishment."

"Oh, are you a believer," he asked.

"Yes," I said.

He told me he attended a Church on the west side and the pastor was the son of the pastor of my Church.

I said, "That's great," and I began to write him a receipt.

All of a sudden he said, "Hey, have you heard of a group of Jews who meet on the west side?"

I said, "Yes, I've heard about it."

He asked, "Have you attended a service?"

I said, "No" (I thought to myself, "I've got a feeling I'm about to").

He went on to say how wonderful their services were and I needed to attend.

I responded by saying; "Maybe soon, I will."

He then said, "Here give me a piece of paper let me write down the name, address and times of services."

He took the paper, wrote down the name, address and times of services. God had answered my prayer! One thing I've learned is if we seek him with all our hearts, truly He will be found and He will answer our prayers. It took me about two more months before I could convince someone to go with me to the West side of town. I didn't want to go alone. I didn't know what this was all about. What was I getting myself into? I was scared. I kept praying telling God I was afraid of this. Please help me not be afraid. God responded.

For the Spirit God gave us does not make us timid, but gives us power, love and self- discipline. [2 Timothy 1:7]

When I first got saved I had asked the Lord to use me where He needed me the most. When I found out we had an enemy, and it was Satan, I wanted to make sure he knew I was on God's side now. I was now determined to surrender my life to God and be used in an area that would be most useful for God's appointed time. I wanted to be used of God where it would be most damaging to Satan. I didn't know what I was committing to at the time, but that was my desire. Sometimes we pray and really don't know what we are praying. For example: when I prayed the above prayer, though I meant it, I didn't know what I was really saying. To totally yield your life to the Lord means your desires have to change and have to line up with what God wants from and for you, and not what we want from God. The cares of this world have to diminish. Your trust in the Lord has to become the ultimate desire to conquer. The Lord reminded me of this verse:

Trust in the Lord with all your heart and lean not on your own understanding; in all your ways submit to Him, and He will make your paths straight. [Proverbs 3:5]

One thing I had learned is the work that God did in me before He called me into His service had to be done. If we don't learn to cleanse our hearts continuously before Him, our hearts will always cause us to miss the mark of God's calling. Our emotions will always get in the way. A stony heart will get in the way of the voice of God.

> *The heart is deceitful above all things and beyond cure. Who can understand it? "I the Lord search the heart and examine the mind, to reward each person according to their conduct, according to what their deeds deserve."* [Jeremiah 17: 9-10]

I've learned when I pray not to assume I am right before God. As I enter His presence I always try to remember to ask him to search my heart and see if there is any offensive way in me. I want to be sure my heart is pure before Him, not perfect, because we all sin and fall short of the glory of God. But certainly we can try to do our best for Him. I call it my spiritual shower. He is so deserving of our best. My sons had gone through so much in our lives I didn't want to make mistakes and take them through things they didn't have to go through. I finally talked my sister Lucila into going to a service at the synagogue with me. It was February 1981 when I first attended a service at what I called a Jewish "Church"—as I called it then.

From Church to a Synagogue

My sister and I went to a service at Kehilat Ben David Messianic Synagogue in El Paso. I had absolutely no idea why God led me to this place, but there seemed to be a breath of God's Spirit or an awakening for Jewish people. Jews were receiving Yeshua as their Messiah and were becoming born again. I didn't understand any of what was going on at most times. I didn't understand what the difference was and why people were so excited. I was confused because Jews were receiving Yeshua. The one thing I held onto was the thought that I had prayed for God to place and use me where He needed me the most. And if this is where God had brought me then I knew He would make things clear in His timing. I began to do more in-depth studying of the Scriptures pertaining to Jewish holidays, Sabbath worship, and the Jewish people, even though I had no understanding of where God was leading me.

There was a lot of turmoil within the Messianic movement back in 1981. But there I was in a synagogue, a divorced gentile with three children. At first I thought I wouldn't last there because everything was so foreign to me. I tried to make some sense of the services but it took time just to feel somewhat comfortable.

My sister continued attending services with me for about a month. We would drop off our kids at a skating rink close by and pick them up after services. I didn't bring my kids because I wanted to be sure of this place. I didn't want to bring my boys into a place I couldn't explain. As I was sitting there trying to enjoy the service and trying to figure out what all this was, it seemed to become more confusing to me. They were reading out of a "Torah." What is a Torah? Why do they do this? And they were dancing in a Church. Was this Biblical? Why were the men wearing "beanies" on their heads? Why were the men wearing a "Talit" and what was that anyway? I had lots to learn.

I began to get involved with the dancing. I loved to dance. Before I came to the Lord, I learned all kinds of dances, from ballroom to African to tap and all kinds of Mexican dances. I just loved to dance. I had been attending services for about two months and now my boys were attending with me. As I got to know the people I felt a little bit more comfortable. Yet, in two months time, there is no way you can know the intensity of a calling. I didn't even know what that meant. As I got more involved I wanted to make sure this was truly where God wanted me to be. Now that I was there, I needed another confirmation. I probably over did it in asking God for confirmation after confirmation.

I went to the Rabbi and told him I needed to leave for a couple of weeks. I told him I wanted to find out if this is truly where God wanted me to be. I felt I was getting emotionally involved with all I was learning and I was also somewhat confused. Especially the dancing, I loved it. I told him I was going to seek the Lord in fasting and prayer and when God answered, I would either be back to stay or I would call him and let him know I would not be returning. Either way, I went away and started to pray for God to please confirm if he wanted me here or not. At this point God was probably listening to me saying, "Oy vey! Here she goes again."

I am a firm believer we should not take a calling lightly. If God calls us to do something, there is always a cost and we need to know it up front in order to be able to say, "Here am I."

I attended services for the next couple of weeks at the Church I had left. Also, my spiritual mother Mama Luke was fasting and praying with me about the synagogue. Though she didn't agree with me leaving and didn't understand the synagogue at the time, she knew I was serious about my walk with the Lord and therefore she joined with me in seeking Him for an answer. A couple of weeks went by and Mama Luke, some other ladies, and I got together for an all night time of prayer. During this time, a lady who I

From Church to a Synagogue

didn't know, came up to me and said she had a word for me. She said, "You are asking the Lord about the ministry He sent you to. He wants you to go back and know that He is with you." I was blown away again at the clear direction God had given me. The lady who gave me the word was a friend of one of regular praying ladies. She knew nothing of what I was fasting and praying for. So that was my answer.

We need to know how to seek a confirmation from the Lord. I have come across people who were angry with God because He let them down. Someone told them God wanted them to do a certain thing and they listened to the person without confirming with God. Especially if it has to do with a drastic life change, you need to hear from God for yourself. After God speaks to you, then pray for conformation and God will confirm what He already told you to do. I'm not saying if someone asks you to do work and help out in your synagogue, you should pray about it. You should always be willing to help out in any way you can. But if it is a calling out of your synagogue or a life-style change, etc., you had better be sure you heard from God and that way you won't be blaming other people for giving you a wrong word. If you seek God, He will answer. The following Friday I went back to the synagogue and spoke to the rabbi and told him I was back to stay.

The synagogue held its main service on Friday evenings. On Saturday mornings there was a short prayer service. I attended all the time. My sons and I attended Bible study during the week and I began to make friends. Concerning the synagogue and Jewish people, I still didn't understand, but I was there to stay. There were lots of Jewish people in the synagogue and I found out there were lots of gentiles, too. And I was one of them. Though I didn't understand what was going on. I noticed as I read the Bible, it made more sense now. I was learning words like, synagogue, Torah, Jews and Law. Though in the Church we didn't study the Old Covenant, I realized the New Covenant of Scripture was making more and more sense to me. I was amazed at the fact the New Covenant was as Jewish as the Old Covenant of Scripture. I had so much to learn.

At this point in time the Jewish men, especially, were trying to figure out what God was saying through all that was happening. There was excitement in the air, as well as confusion in God's camp. Jews were trying to go back to being Jewish (whatever that meant) and now there were gentiles, adding to the confusion. And I was as confused as anybody. At least being Jewish, you knew you belonged there, but what about me? What was I doing there?

When we started attending, there were Jews married to Gentiles. The question was, how do we handle this if the Scriptures teach no intermarriage? What do they do with the Gentiles in the synagogue? Much was going on and there were so many questions and so many fears for those of us who were there. I was only there in obedience to God and for no other known reason. Months back, I didn't even know of the existence of Jews or Israel. How could this be? I continued to fast and pray because I needed the presence of God with me as I walked in this messianic life on a daily basis. Remember, I had three boys to consider, but God continued to assure me of His calling in my life.

As I continued to hear the Rabbi's teachings, I had to go home and study what he was saying. As a Gentile, I needed to seek the Lord and Scripture to find out what my obligation to God and the Jews were.

> *Again I ask: Did Israel not understand? First, Moses says, "I will make you envious by those who are not a nation; I will make you angry by a nation that has no understanding." And Isaiah boldly says, "I was found by those who did not seek me; I revealed myself to those who did not ask for me." [Romans 10:19-20]*

Was I supposed to make Israel envious? How? What does this mean? How could someone like me make anyone envious about anything?

First of all, I was just now getting to know these people. Finding out Yeshua—who saved me—was Jewish, and all the questions I had asked my pastor about the Passover and other issues were being answered by celebrating the actual events was confusing. I had been told that these celebrations had been done away with the Old Covenant writings. Who was right? What was difficult at the time was I had no one to go to for answers except the Lord.

What does it mean to make Israel envious by those who are not a nation? I had been told not to share Yeshua with Jews. I had been taught the holidays mentioned in the New Covenant Scriptures were no longer valid and active. And yet I read Yeshua and His disciples were celebrating these holidays. Who was right? I had to find the answer in the Scriptures. In all my Scripture readings, I had never read where God said to stop celebrating the appointed feasts of the Lord.

> *Get rid of the old yeast, so that you may be a new unleavened batch—as you really are. For Messiah, our Passover lamb, has been sacrificed. Therefore let us keep the Festival, not with the old bread leavened with malice and wickedness, but with the unleavened bread of sincerity and truth.* [1 Corinthians 5:7-8]

As I continued to study Scripture, I began to see the Old Covenant and New Covenant had to be taught together. *Leviticus 23:2* instructed Moses in this way:

> *"Speak to the Israelites and say to them: "These are My appointed festivals, the appointed festivals of the Lord, which you are to proclaim as sacred assemblies."* [Leviticus 23:2]

These were the appointed feasts of the Lord, not of Israel. God had commanded Israel to follow these in obedience to Him.

As I continued learning, I was dealing with the rejection of who I was, as a Gentile. At times I went through the emotions of thinking I was crazy for being there. I would share all I was learning with my Christians friends and everyone thought I was crazy. Jewish people were so busy trying to figure out what was going on with them; they had no time or energy to give thought to the Gentile sitting next to them in the synagogue. There was no one I could turn to for help except God Himself.

CALL OF A GENTILE / LEARNING JEWISH CULTURE

There was so much excitement in the synagogue all the time. The music was different, but beautiful. I didn't understand the reading of the Hebrew Scriptures—it was never taught in my previous Church experiences—but it brought tears to my eyes. I was now sitting in a synagogue worshiping with the Jews and learning Yeshua was Jewish and they were God's chosen people. All I was learning about the Jewish people always brought tears to my eyes. When I was about 11-years-old, my mother bought a television set. I was a Catholic at the time. That first movie I watched on T.V. was Yeshua of Nazareth. I didn't know Yeshua was the Son of God. All I had been told was the Man on the cross was God. The first time I watched the movie, seeing Him hurt as He carried the cross, I went and leaned onto the television screen and cried. I told Yeshua, "I am so sorry you hurt so much, if I had been there I would've helped you." Every year the movie was shown I repeated the same words. As I got older I would say to Him, "I wish I had been part of your people." I didn't know what I was saying at the time—so many years earlier—but here I was now in the midst of His people. If only I knew how to fit in. But I knew God would show me as I continued to trust Him.

One Friday evening I was helping clean the kitchen after Oneg. Three Jewish ladies were still in the kitchen finishing up whatever they were doing. The service was about to start and I heard one on them say, "We need to shut the lights and go to the sanctuary; call a goy." And they started laughing. I didn't know what goy meant at the time. But one of them called me over and said, "Hey Irene, the sun is going down would you come here and shut the lights off?" So I went over and shut the lights. As they walked away laughing, I just thought they were happy. One of my friends heard them and came up to me. He was upset with me because I shut the lights for the ladies. He asked me why I had listened to them. I told him I didn't mind shutting lights off. I asked why he was so upset and he told me the word goy was a derogatory word for gentile, and they were doing this to make fun of me.

Other situations happened. I was asked to have a meeting with several people, including four Jewish ladies. I was called into the office and the meeting began with one of the ladies telling me they wanted to make sure I understood, even though I was at a synagogue, I was not allowed to marry a Jewish man. "Gentiles were forbidden to marry Jewish men" she said. I didn't understand why they needed to hold a meeting to inform me of their worry. After all, I was not there to find a husband, and at the time I had no intentions of marriage.

They expressed other concerns because I was divorced and had Gentile children. One of them said, "You have to know marriage for you to a Jewish man would never work."

I was confused and hurt at what they were saying to me, but I assured all of them I was not there to look for a husband. But if God had a Jewish man for me to marry, God would choose him and he would be a man who would do what God instructed him, and he would not be afraid of what men thought about it. This was not mentioned again. It was at times like this I wanted to leave so badly, but God would not let me.

My feelings were hurt because they continued to treat me so badly. Anytime they needed something they would make the comment of the goy and call me over. I remembered Yeshua said we were supposed to be servants of all. I told my friend that if this was the worst of my service to them, I was willing to do it as unto the Lord. I find in Churches and synagogues people are always getting their feelings hurt. We need to grow in the likeness of our Messiah and serve and do all things unto Him. Yes, what they were doing to me was not nice, and I'm sure God wasn't pleased with it, but you have to understand that most of these women were babies in the Lord and what they were doing was showing who they were at the time. It takes time for all of us to grow in the likeness of the Messiah. And, again, I want to mention if the Lord had not taken me through the process of healing and forgiveness before I came to the synagogue, I would not have been ready for this. So many of us have never taken the time to develop our security of who we are in Yeshua and therefore our insecurities get in the way of what God wants to do through us.

At this time, Jews were trying to seek God to find the movement's identity and some direction. It was like they were ready to come out of the wilderness. The Scriptures were coming alive to the Jewish community. But what was God saying? I listened to different conversations at the beginning of the Messianic movement, and I kept thinking: If the Jews aren't sure of all God was saying, how was I to know what to do?

The more I prayed, the more I heard the Lord say: "Trust Me and be still and learn all you need to learn." These are the times you need to be sure of what He is doing through you or what He has called you to do. I had many doubts, but I prayed them away by using the Word of God. I leaned on this verse:

> *Trust in the Lord with all your heart and lean not on your own understanding; in all your ways submit to Him, and He will make your paths straight.* [Proverbs 3:5-6]

As I continued learning about the Jewish Messiah, I wanted everyone to know Him in the manner I was getting to know Him. It is so different to be saved by Yeshua and then to learn how to walk with Him as the Jewish Messiah—the Anointed One—the one Moses spoke about and to understand that Yeshua fulfilled the writings of the Prophets.

> *"Do not think that I have come to abolish the Law or the Prophets; I have not come to abolish them but to fulfill them. For truly I tell you, until heaven and earth disappear, not the smallest letter, not the least stroke of a pen, will by any means disappear from the Law until everything is accomplished. Therefore anyone who sets aside one of the least of these commands and teaches others accordingly*

will be called least in the kingdom of heaven, but whoever practices and teaches these commands will be called great in the kingdom of heaven. For I tell you that unless your righteousness surpasses that of the Pharisees and the teachers of the law, you will certainly not enter the kingdom of heaven." [Matthew 5:17-20]

Often I hear the word "fulfill" defined as done away with. The definition of fulfill is: to bring into actuality, to put into effect. If we continue to define this Scripture as saying the Law has been done away with, we will miss what Yeshua came to do besides bring total salvation to each one of us. There is nothing greater for us to know than we have been atoned for and that our names are written in the Lamb's Book of Life. Even though I couldn't find anyone to share what I was learning according to the Scriptures, I continued to study on my own.

20

SAVED BY JESUS / WALKING WITH YESHUA

I continued learning about this Jewish Messiah and all He was besides my Savior. I wanted everyone to know Him as I was getting to know Him. I began to call Him by His Hebrew name "Yeshua" which means salvation.

When Yeshua first appeared in *John 1:45*, Philip found Nathanael and told him, "*We have found the One Moses wrote about in the Law, and about whom the prophets also wrote- Yeshua of Nazareth, the son of Joseph*." Even though we call Him by His English name, He never commissioned the disciples or anyone else to remove His Jewish identification. I believe this is a big part of the confusion we have today in so many Churches. Many people say they believe in Yeshua. But if I ask you to introduce Him to me, how would you describe Him? What do you know about Him as a person? Yeshua walked in Israel in a fleshly body, had a Jewish mother (Miriam) and a Jewish father (Yosef). Because of the title given to Yeshua as the Jewish Messiah, Messianic Jew is a title for those who have embraced Yeshua and are born again in accordance to *John 3:3*. He never meant to change forms of worship into something other than what the disciples were teaching.

Now there were staying in Jerusalem God-fearing Jews from every nation under heaven. When they heard this sound, a crowd came together in bewilderment, because each one heard their own language being spoken. Utterly amazed, they asked: "Aren't all these who are speaking Galileans? Then how is it that each of us hears them in our native language? Parthians, Medes and Elamites; residents of Mesopotamia, Judea and Cappadocia, Pontus and Asia, Phrygia and Pamphylia, Egypt and the parts of Libya near Cyrene; visitors from Rome (both Jews and converts to Judaism); Cretans and Arabs—we hear them declaring the wonders of God in our own tongues!" Amazed and perplexed, they asked one another, "What does this mean?" [Acts 2:5-12]

Then Barnabas went to Tarsus to look for Saul, and when he found him, he brought him to Antioch. So for a whole year Barnabas and Saul met with the church and taught great numbers of people. The disciples were called Christians first at Antioch. [Acts 11:25-26]

Why were there converts to Judaism? What is Judaism? Webster's Dictionary defines Judaism: "The monotheistic religion of the Jewish people, tracing its origins to Abraham and having its spiritual and ethical principles embodied chiefly in the Bible and the Talmud. It is conformity to the traditional ceremonies and rites of the Jewish religion the cultural and spiritual and social way of life of the Jewish people."

The Lord or the disciples never taught the nations the "Good News" while doing away with Jewish practices. The word Christian means: "one who lives according to the teachings of Yeshua." What did Yeshua teach?

When I began to study the Bible connecting the Old Covenant to the New Covenant and referencing the New Covenant to prophesy in the Old Covenant, everything began to make sense. For example, this is one of the most important commands the God of Abraham told Moses to give the Israelites:

Hear, O Israel: The Lord our God, the Lord is one. Love the Lord your God with all your heart and with all your soul and with all your strength. These commandments that I give you today are to be on your hearts. Impress them on your children. Talk about them when you sit at home and when you walk along the road, when you lie down and when you get up. Tie them as symbols on your hands and bind them on your foreheads. Write them on the doorframes of your houses and on your gates. [Deuteronomy 6:4-9]

When Yeshua was asked about the most important commandment He made the answer very clear to the Pharisees.

One of the teachers of the law came and heard them debating. Noticing that Yeshua had given them a good answer, He asked him, "Of all the commandments, which is the most important?"

"The most important one," answered Yeshua, "is this: "Hear, O Israel: The Lord our God, the Lord is one. Love the Lord your God with all your heart and with all your soul and with all your mind and with all your strength." The second is this: "Love your neighbor as yourself. There is no commandment greater than these." [Mark 12:28-31]

To this day religious Jews and all Messianic Jews recite this command. I ask you to think about this: If Yeshua proclaimed this commandment as the most important; shouldn't we Gentiles pay closer attention to it? And since the Law is the main focus and subject of scrutiny in this section of Mark, why do people insist the Law has been done away with? I believe people need to re-think this viewpoint.

Before I knew all this about Judaism, I didn't understand the significance when I saw religious Jews wearing "Tefillin." I didn't know the Scripture said to literally tie them as symbols on your hands and bind them on your foreheads. I know only the very religious Jews do this, but they are actually following a command. Also, there was the instruction of writing them on the doorframes of your houses and on your gates. When you go to a Jewish home you will see what is called a "Mezuzah" on the doorpost of the doors. This Mezuzah also has the Word of God in it. It is kissed as you leave the house and when you return. You do this to always remember God is with you all the time. As a Gentile, I was so excited to be learning all these things. Now my question at the time was this: I am not Jewish, so what does all this mean to me?

After I had been in the synagogue for a while, everyone, for the most part, knew I was there to stay. I had proven I loved the Lord and I was serious about being there. I began to help more and more, but I still had questions about my role in the synagogue. What am I suppose to be doing? Am I here to be a servant to the Jewish people? I continued to sit and learn all I could about the Jewish culture. After all, Yeshua was a Jew and He lived as a Jew. I wanted to know more and more. One thing I knew for sure: I was called to follow the Jewish carpenter Messiah Yeshua. Being raised a Mexican, in a Mexican culture, was all I knew at the time, but what did this mean for my Gentile children and me? My children would ask me questions about the synagogue and the services there, "Why do they do this or that?" I tried to find some answers to explain, but still I would get confused about what we were doing there.

One evening as I was praying and asking the Lord to show me how to talk to my boys about the synagogue and he led me to read the Gospels again. I realized Yeshua always went to teach in the synagogues. I was in a synagogue and this is where I was learning about who Yeshua was. I answered my children by reading Scripture to them and I stopped trying to interpret. I had been taught the Passover was no longer celebrated, and now here we were celebrating Passover as Yeshua and all the writers of Scripture did. There were no longer questions about Passover; I was following a command given by the God of Abraham, Isaac and Jacob as He had commanded Moses to instruct the Israelites.

> *The Lord said to Moses, "Speak to the Israelites and say to them: 'These are My appointed festivals, the appointed festivals of the Lord, which you are to proclaim as sacred assemblies.'"* [Leviticus 23:1-2]

Moses goes on to mention and give direction on all the feasts the Lord had instructed, from honoring the Sabbath, Passover, Firstfruits, Feasts of Weeks, Feasts of Trumpets, Day of Atonement and the Feast of Tabernacles. I wanted to know what the Scriptures said for me to do as a Gentile. Exodus states this about Passover:

> *"This is a day you are to commemorate; for the generations to come you shall celebrate it as a festival to the Lord — a lasting ordinance."* [Exodus 12:14]

> *"For seven days no yeast is to be found in your houses. And anyone, whether foreigner or native-born, who eats anything with yeast in it must be cut off from the community of Israel. Eat nothing made with yeast. Wherever you live, you must eat unleavened bread."* [Exodus 12:19-20]

Some people confuse the Feasts of the Lord with the commands given to Israel as a nation. For example, there is discussion of the commandment of circumcision. I've had people say to me that the Jews no longer need circumcision. In *Acts 15*, you will read all that was discussed concerning the Gentiles, the Law and Circumcision. In *Acts 15:29* the Scriptures say:

> *You are to abstain from food sacrificed to idols, from blood, from the meat of strangled animals and from sexual immorality. You will do well to avoid these things.*

The Apostles were not imposing circumcision onto the Gentiles. Even though, in the years being in a Messianic Synagogue, there have been Gentile families that chose to circumcise their newborn males as a sign of commitment and connection to Israel. This still does not make a Gentile a physical Jew nor is this a requirement in order to be part of a Messianic Synagogue. A Gentile person is accepted with the same love. Jews and Gentiles work together with understanding in order to bring about God's will for the salvation of the world and the redemption of the Jewish people.

As I continued to study Old Covenant Scriptures and connected it to the New Covenant, it was becoming clear. What does Passover have to do with the New Covenant writings? I found out in the Book of John, it was during the third Passover celebration that Yeshua was celebrating with His disciples, when He was arrested.

> *Then came the day of Unleavened Bread on which the Passover lamb had to be sacrificed.* [Luke 22:7]
>
> *They left and found things just as Yeshua had told them. So they prepared the Passover. When the hour came, Yeshua and His apostles reclined at the table. And He said to them,*
>
> *"I have eagerly desired to eat this Passover with you before I suffer. For I tell you, I will not eat it again until it finds fulfillment in the kingdom of God."* [Luke 22:13-16]

I encourage everyone to study the Scriptures concerning Passover and the feasts.

> *It was the day of Preparation of the Passover; it was about noon. "Here is your king," Pilate said to the Jews.* [John 19:14]

This is just one scripture that mentions Passover as the time when Yeshua was arrested, crucified and then raised from the dead on the Feast of Firstfruits.

I realized as a Gentile I had missed so much by the mere fact the feasts were not taught in the Churches. I found out the Holy Spirit was given during the Feasts of Weeks, which is also known as Shavuot or Pentecost. That's why Yeshua told His disciples to go to Jerusalem and wait for the gift the Father had promised. Shavuot had to connect to Yeshua.

With The Feast of Trumpets, we read about a trumpet being blown, which could usher in the second coming of Yeshua (otherwise known as "the rapture"). How about the Day of Atonement and the Feast of Tabernacles? All these questions were being answered as I sat and learned from the rabbi and others around me. I was so excited to be able to share all I was learning with my Christian friends. At the time, all I would get was: "That's good, I'm glad you're happy."

As I continued to learn more I realized the feasts were documented and celebrated in the New Covenant Scriptures, from Yeshua to the disciples to the beloved Apostle Paul. In fact, Paul tells us Passover is to be celebrated as he mentions yeast in the Scripture.

> *Your boasting is not good. Don't you know that a little yeast leavens the whole batch of dough? Get rid of the old yeast, so that you may be a new unleavened batch—as you really are. For Messiah, our Passover lamb, has been sacrificed. Therefore let us keep the Festival, not with the old bread leavened with malice and wickedness, but with the unleavened bread of sincerity and truth.* [1 Corinthians 5:6-8]

How was I to grasp and understand what all this meant if I didn't celebrate Passover? Paul is pretty straight forward when he wrote, "*Therefore let us keep the Festival.*" I had been taught that all this had been done away with, but here is the great Apostle Paul instructing the Church in Corinth about keeping the Passover with new understanding. No one was able to show me any Scripture where God—or any of Yeshua's disciples—said that the Feasts of the Lord were obsolete.

I had been in the synagogue for about three years now. Since I was a single parent and an older woman in comparison to the younger women who were attending, I began to help counsel them. I was teaching them how to learn to follow Yeshua and find security in our precious Messiah. Most of these younger ladies wanted a husband but at this point of their lives had no desire to serve God in any other way. I remember reading a book about relationships and the need for Jewish men to marry Jewish women. I was fine with the concept because I wasn't interested in marriage at the time. I was there to serve God and find out how I could be of service at the synagogue.

People would ask me how I could continue to stay there with so much conflict that was taking place at the time. Questions like, do we keep kosher? What about intermarriage? What about those Jews who were already married to Gentiles? There were so many questions. All I could do is continue to seek and spend time with the Lord. I made up my mind I would continue to grow in His likeness because that is what He instructed me to do. The Scripture tell us we are saved and to be conformed to His image.

I always believe if I find favor with God, He will give me favor with men. That is His promise. I continued to adhere to my conviction this was where the Lord had called me and I was going to concentrate on learning all He wanted to teach me. Besides, the more I learned the more I loved the Jewish people. I began to really understand all that the nation of Israel had gone through to bring forth our precious Yeshua and all the wrong that had been done to the Jewish people in the Name of Yeshua. The nation of Israel went through so much because they are the chosen ones who were called to suffer in order to bring about God's plan of redemption for the world.

When referring to God's chosen people some will ask: "Are you saying the Jews are more special to God than I am?" The answer is no—they are not special in that sense. However, they are certainly chosen to be the nation and the people of whom the God of Abraham will fulfill his plan. From the beginning God chose a nation to bring about Messiah Yeshua. Yeshua put it this way.

"You Samaritans worship what you do not know; we worship what we do know, for salvation is from the Jews." [John 4:22]

Yeshua is including himself by using the word "we" and therefore saying we Jews know what we worship. I realized if we Gentiles continued to teach the New Covenant without the awareness of its connection to the Old Covenant, we would never get the whole and correct picture of what God was doing and His calling on our lives. More and more I began to notice things that were alarming or not quite complete. For example: some T-shirts or other Christian items were sold with this abbreviated version of Romans 1:16: *"For I am not ashamed of the Good News, because it is the power of God that brings salvation to everyone who believes…"*

I realized every print that had gone out making this statement of salvation was incomplete. To this date things haven't changed. The entire verse reads:

For I am not ashamed of the Good News, because it is the power of God that brings salvation to everyone who believes: first to the Jew, then to the Gentile. [Romans 1:16]

Why has this been allowed? Was Yeshua only referring to the Book of Revelation when He said?

I warn everyone who hears the words of the prophecy of this scroll: If anyone adds anything to them, God will add to that person the plagues described in this scroll. And if anyone takes words away from this scroll of prophecy, God will take away from that person any share in the tree of life and in the Holy City, which are described in this scroll. [Revelation 22:18-19]

The above-mentioned Scripture in the Book of Romans is just one example. We need to do it right and in accordance to what God wrote not what people want to hear. I was surprised that some Church leaders were allowing this to be printed, as it was excluding *"first to the Jew, then to the Gentile."* When I would mention this to friends and other Christians the usual response was: "What's the big deal with the Jew?" I would answer them by saying the Jewish people were a big deal because God would use the nation of Israel and the Jewish people in His final plan. I noticed people would get jealous because of the word "chosen" and some would argue with me so I would include more Scripture.

There will be trouble and distress for every human being who does evil: first for the Jew, then for the Gentile; but glory, honor and peace for everyone who does good: first for the Jew, then for the Gentile. For God does not show favoritism. [Romans 2:9-11]

It was hard to teach Jews and Gentiles are spiritually bonded, but Israel and the Jewish people are chosen for a specific purpose in God's plan. I continued in the synagogue and helping where I was needed. I began reading books about the sufferings of the Jewish people at the hands of people who referred to themselves as "Christians." One great book I read was "Our Hands Are Stained with Blood" by Dr. Michael Brown.

I could not believe how much damage had been done to the Jewish people and how far we, as the body of the Messiah, had withdrawn from our Jewish roots. I taught my sons about Biblical Judaism. I would share what I was learning with all my family and friends and held studies with them regarding the Jewish roots of the faith. I was excited to share with everyone that Yeshua was Jewish, and the mother of Yeshua, whom I had grown up worshiping, was a Jewish woman chosen by the God of Abraham to give birth to our beloved Messiah. The Bible was a Jewish book!

I began to live a Biblically Jewish lifestyle and I began to keep kosher as best as possible. We celebrated Chanukah instead of Christmas. Because my family and friends still celebrated Christmas, I would come over to their homes and use the opportunity to share the Jewish Messiah with them. God showed me how to use what I was learning to teach in love and not to condemn or judge. I found such joy in my walk with the Lord and felt so privileged to have been chosen to learn the truth about the faith's Jewish roots. Needless to say, I lost most of my friends because they couldn't understand me anymore. But that was okay, because after 4½ years of being in the synagogue, I knew this was to be a life-long journey with Messiah. I wasn't sure what it all meant. All I wanted was to walk with the Jewish Messiah every day of my life. I would study every chance I got during lunch break at work, and at night after I had my reading and prayers with my children. Nothing in the world gave me more joy than to spend time in the Word and with Messiah Yeshua.

21

Ruth and Boaz

There was a man—a Jewish man—in the synagogue and he was the right-hand man to the rabbi. Because I helped with counseling, I became part of the leadership in that area. We all got to know each other more and more as we attended meetings together. We all had lunch together and he and I were also part of the dance team in the synagogue. After 4½ years everyone knew my walk with the Lord was solid and I was there to do whatever God would have me to do. In other words, I had proven myself to my rabbi and others. I was not there to play games. I was there to help and serve God.

We used to have services on Friday nights and Saturday mornings and my boys and I always attended. By now my boys loved the synagogue. God had given us peace and joy since He called us to be there. One Friday evening service, as we were worshiping, I caught myself staring at this Jewish man—something I had never done before. This caught me by surprise. I asked the Lord for forgiveness and I continued to praise. In a couple of minutes I caught myself staring at him again. I quickly asked the Lord, "What is going on? Why is this happening?" The Lord spoke to me and said, "He is going to be your husband."

I was shocked and embarrassed. Shocked because I had not entertained the thought of marriage, and embarrassed because I thought everyone had seen I had been staring at this man. Needless to say when I got home that night, and after making sure my sons were in bed, I immediately went to spend my time with the Lord. I asked him for forgiveness again for staring and asked him to show me what was happening. The Lord spoke to me again and said, "Yossi is going to be your husband."

I was shocked! How can this be? I was a divorced woman raising three sons. Yossi was a single man, the right-hand man to the rabbi. Was I crazy? Besides I didn't want to cause problems. I was there to help. I told the Lord if this was Him speaking, He had to reveal what He wanted to do because I wasn't telling a soul and I was especially not mentioning this to Yossi.

A couple of weeks went by and the congregation was going through some rough adjustment times. Some of us decided to go on a fast and to pray for God's direction for the synagogue. I went on a fast and prayed as I had never prayed before. Yossi had decided to go away for a few days to seek the Lord. I knew he had gone away because it was mentioned in a meeting. At this time, I had not mentioned to anyone, what the Lord had said to me about him. Again I said to the Lord, "If this is you, you have to speak to him and confirm to me." I am not taking one step nor am I saying one word to anyone. I did ask my spiritual mother (Mama Luke) to fast and pray with me about a serious situation, but did not mention what it was. Yossi had gone to the Gila Wilderness in Silver City, New Mexico to seek the Lord and when he came back, he was a changed man. You could see the peace of God in him.

I began to study the book of Ruth. The reason I decided to do this was because someone had told me that the intermarriage teaching was incorrect because of Ruth. Who was Ruth?

How did she respond to Naomi? I had lots of questions about Ruth.

Several times I'll hear people say, "The Lord said," but in fact it winds up as only emotional or fleshly desires. I did not want that to happen to me. I had much to lose if this was the case. As I started studying the book of Ruth, I realized Gentiles use this phrase without understanding the impact of the life of Ruth. Ruth gave her life to take care of her mother-in- law. She was willing to leave her family, her culture and all she knew to become one who would take care of her mother-in-law until death.

But Ruth replied, "Don't urge me to leave you or to turn back from you. Where you go I will go, and where you stay I will stay. Your people will be my people and your God my God. Where you die I will die, and there I will be buried. May the Lord deal with me, be it ever so severely, if even death separates you and me." When Naomi realized that Ruth was determined to go with her, she stopped urging her. [Ruth 1:16-18]

When you study Ruth you realize it cost her all she knew in order to become who God wanted her to be. The more I read and studied the more scared I got because, after all, how was I going to raise my sons? How could I possibly do this? This meant there was no turning back to my family and to all I had known. It's a scary thought when God calls you and you know what He has asked you to do can only be done by miracles. The more I considered the cost, the more I was determined to do nothing until God moved.

One thing I learned is to be a "Ruth" means you understand the Jewish people and you have realized the plan of God through the promise made to Abraham. So many people use the phrase: "I'm a Ruth, and therefore there is no difference between me and a Jew." I'm here to tell you there is a great difference in just being one by name and being a "Ruth" by lifestyle.

By the time I got done studying Ruth, I realized God was saying to me: I would marry into a Jewish lifestyle and I would continue to raise my sons knowing the Jewish Messiah. I finally said "Yes" to the Lord, but I still continued to wait.

A couple of weeks went by and Yossi found out my birthday was near. He came to me after Shabbat service and asked if he could take me out to dinner for my birthday. At first I was reluctant to go because I kept thinking it wasn't right. He insisted, and I finally agreed. The following Saturday evening he picked me up and took me out to dinner at "Billy Crews Steakhouse." This was a really expensive place. My first thought was, "Hmm, too cozy of a place for friends to have dinner." But I gave it no other thought after that. I hadn't been to a place like this since I came to know the Lord. I had not dated and I couldn't afford the restaurant on my own, so I was determined to enjoy the evening. I think I ordered everything on the menu.

Yossi was such a gentleman and he made me feel so free. We had become good friends and I was now getting to know him as a man of God in other areas. We had a great time together and we talked about our past. He told me everything about himself before he came to know the Lord, and I shared my whole life story with him as well.

About a week later, Yossi called me and asked me if I would go with him to a dinner that was being given at another nice restaurant. His company awarded him the "President's Award" and they were honoring him with a dinner and a gift. So he didn't want to go alone. We went to dinner and had a wonderful time together.

I realized we were both enjoying spending time together. Yossi was always mature and responsible at the synagogue and I never noticed him flirting with women. He dressed very nice and helped the rabbi with whatever he needed. I liked those qualities in him.

After our second dinner date as friends, I decided to have a talk with him. I told him as much as I enjoyed his company, I couldn't risk any talk about us. I asked him why he had decided to ask me out to dinner for my birthday and now another event. I told him that as much as I appreciated the dinners and the good-clean fun we had together, I couldn't continue doing this because it might give a different appearance to others. And besides, I had to think about my sons' feelings as well.

Yossi told me he began having feelings for me after he came back from the Gila wilderness. He said he had gone up to seek the Lord because he wanted God's will for his life and wanted to make a difference for God. I asked him what that meant. He said he would like to pray about starting a relationship with me. When he said that, I began to cry and told him what the Lord had said to me. I told him I still thought this was crazy. I told him to really pray because getting married to a divorced woman was a very hard thing. I told him everything I was going through with my sons and he needed to be sure this was God, because my life was hard.

We continued to pray for God's direction. Yossi talked to my sons and told them how he wanted to marry me and help them. My youngest son didn't like Yossi or any other man in my life. He was very jealous. At the time this was happening, there was much division and strife in the synagogue. Remember, this was the beginning of the new awakening of Messianic Judaism and the teachings were: Don't marry a Gentile.

We both knew the Lord was doing this, but we knew our rabbi would not be in agreement with the idea. Yossi and I went to speak to David Katz, who was one of our best friends and in leadership in the synagogue. We told him what had happened and we wanted to start a relationship towards marriage. Yossi and David decided they would go talk to the rabbi.

It was no surprise the rabbi was against the relationship right from the start. He and others in the Messianic movement had preached Jews should not marry Gentiles. So there we were and I kept thinking: Am I being disobedient to God? As we were going through this I studied more and discovered there has always been Gentiles in the midst of Israel (Jews). But the one thing that is so often missed is they were walking with and becoming part of Israel. I don't believe there is anything wrong with a Messianic Jew marrying a Messianic Gentile, but they must be sure God is calling them to do this. The focus for marriage is to work together for the kingdom of God. Not to say that all other aspects of attraction are not important, but we need to continue to remember our lives are not ours to do as we please, but we are here to please Yeshua. Your partner has to be someone with the same vision and the same understanding of God's calling.

Our Rabbi at the time didn't allow and would not perform a mixed marriage. I was very hurt over this. I thought I had proven myself in my walk with the Lord and I had become a servant to all. Our rabbi would not talk to me. He had asked Yossi to keep this a secret and he would let us know when he was going to announce our relationship.

Yossi and I wanted to do this in an orderly and Scriptural manner. I had to really work hard searching my heart. Because of the teachings regarding Jews and Gentiles, I needed to make sure I wasn't acting with the wrong intentions and I wasn't trying to prove anyone wrong with an "I'll show them" attitude. I couldn't afford to make a mistake over this. Also, I had been told by other Jewish people in the synagogue I couldn't marry a Jewish man. The comments went like this: "Besides you already have children so there is no way a marriage here would work for you."

Much of the strife the synagogue was experiencing at the time, had to do with hurt and misunderstandings. Gentiles were crying during services because they felt like they didn't belong. We had the issues of Jewish men married to Gentile women and Jewish women married to Gentile men.

Because of the new awakening of Messianic movement and the Jewish rabbis trying to figure out what God was saying, there were lots of mistakes made. We all had so many areas in which we needed to seek God.

Yossi and I talked and prayed a lot because of some many different circumstances. The synagogue became such a place of contention. Gentiles wives were getting upset with their Jewish husbands and Gentile husbands were getting upset with their Jewish wives. Needless to say, we were facing some serious issues. Yossi was always an honest and responsible man, especially in the matters of his walk with the Lord; after all, he was the rabbi's right-hand man. What the Lord was doing with us was hard for everyone, so we decided we had to let someone else know what was happening in our lives, especially after time went on and the rabbi would not bless our relationship. So we submitted ourselves to our great friend David Katz again.

I want to make something clear here. The time period I am talking about took place about 30 years ago. This was the beginning of the new wave of Messianic Judaism. The rabbi wanted to be sure he was following God's direction. He had taught he would not marry a Jew and a Gentile. He was following his conviction at the time. I don't want to come across as if I'm trying to defame our rabbi. I am a firm believer every relationship should begin in prayer with your rabbi or someone in leadership in the synagogue. Even though our rabbi did not want to acknowledge our relationship, Yossi and I knew this was God's will. The teaching of Jews not marrying Gentiles stems from the fact that if a Jew marries a Gentile, he or she winds up leaving the God of Israel and turning to other gods. This was the fear.

The Lord is calling his Jewish people back to Himself and restoring His Messianic Kingdom. Therefore if you are thinking of marriage, be sure you pray for someone that has the same vision and calling.

So here we were, Yossi and I, trying to make sense of what God was telling us to do. We both became very hurt and frustrated with our rabbi, but we tried to adhere to what he was asking of us: not to share our relationship with anyone.

Yossi and I began to go out to eat together. He began coming over to my apartment to spend time with my sons. He talked to my sons and told them about his interest in me, and he believed God wanted us to get married. He wanted them to know he would try very hard to be there for them.

I knew how hard it was to raise children. At times I would try to talk Yossi into not marrying me because I knew how hard it would be for us.

At this time Alex was already out of the house. Paul was 17 and Michael was 12. I believed Yossi was getting into something he did not understand. But this was a man who would do whatever God told him and remain steady no matter how hard things got. That is one thing I always admired about him. He was always at synagogue early and made sure all things were ready to go and in order. He was always the last one to leave, making sure all things were secured. To this day he remains the steady, committed person I married.

A situation happened at the synagogue that caused us to make the decision to go public with our relationship. A Jewish young man and a Jewish young lady decided to start a relationship towards marriage. They had just decided to start dating and the rabbi brought them to the front of the synagogue during a Shabbat service and announced their relationship and blessed it. It had been at least a couple of months since Yossi had gone to the rabbi and shared about us starting a relationship, and up to this point, he had not mentioned it to anybody. I think the rabbi was hoping it would just go away. When the rabbi blessed this other couple, after much prayer and accountability to the rest of the leadership, we decided it was time to go public with our relationship.

There was a big commotion about it. The Jewish people were upset with me, the Gentiles were happy this happened. The rabbi still wouldn't talk to me about any of it. I was so hurt by him. There was a time when I began to think this couldn't be from the Lord and I kept saying to the Lord, "If this is from you, how can this be so difficult?" Because of everything that was happening, I began to doubt. I told Yossi I was going on a fast to seek God because I was not going on with this until God Himself came down and confirmed this was Him.

I went on a fast and had spoken to my spiritual mother about fasting with me for God's answer. At this point I had been at the synagogue 4 ½ years and did nothing to cause question about my walk with the Lord and my intention to serve. Still the rabbi had not yet talked to me. I told the Lord and Yossi that unless God Himself came down and confirmed this relationship, I would not walk the aisle in marriage. You can only imagine the confusion in what I heard God saying and what the rabbi was teaching. Also having to deal with all the animosity I had against the rabbi. In my quiet time at night God would reassure me of His leading in this ordeal.

I continued to fast and pray. We used to have Bible study on Tuesday nights, and during the second week of my fast, we had a woman from a ministry in Florida come and do a teaching on worship. When she finished with the teaching, there was a silence as she asked the rabbi for permission to wait on the Lord because she felt God was not finished for the evening (waiting on the Spirit). There was silence as we all were waiting.

I was sitting on the right-side middle and was blocked from seeing upfront because someone was sitting in front of me. A couple of minutes went by and still the silence remained.

I decided to lean to the side because I wanted to see what was going on upfront. As I leaned to the side to take a look, the woman saw me and signaled me to come up. I was shocked that upon seeing me, she signaled me to come forward. I went up to the front and she began to pray for me. She then went on to say, "You have been asking God about a relationship you are in. God wants you to know this is of Him and He will be with you in all you have to go through." She said this song is for you, she sang "The Battle Belongs to the Lord." At the end, she gave me a big hug and said, "And when you see Marilyn tell her how much God loves her." As I was walking back to my seat, she turned to the rabbi and said to him, "The Lord is done here." I was the only one she ministered to that night. I had never seen this lady before. She didn't know me and I didn't know her. And by the way, Marilyn was Yossi's mother's name. God showed up!

When I asked the Lord to confirm our relationship, I was not going to accept a confirmation from my spiritual mother nor from anyone else who knew what was going on. I knew how real God is and I was sure He would answer and I just had to wait on Him. Again, I couldn't afford to make a mistake. I had promised the Lord if He showed me this was Him, I would do whatever, no matter what, and trust Him with my sons.

Things began to turn around and the rabbi called Yossi and I into his office. We had a long talk and he finally apologized for what he had done. He asked me if I would allow him to marry us. At this point I was at a place where he would be the last person I would want to marry us. But because I knew God was working in this, I was honest with him and told him I didn't want him to perform our wedding. I told him I knew this was something that extended beyond us, and though I didn't want him to do it, I knew he was the one God had chosen to perform the ceremony. I told him I was very angry, but I was going to believe by the date we were to get married, God would heal my heart and there would be restoration in all of us.

Yossi and I got married on March 2, 1985. Yossi adopted my son Michael the first year of our marriage. Our sons Alex and Paul were now older so they kept their last name. Alex and Paul live and work in El Paso, Texas. Our son Michael works as a personal trainer and is working towards opening a healthy food restaurant. Paul works in a restaurant and is working to get back into the hair cutting business. For those of you that would question why I address all my sons as OUR children, it's because Yossi assumed responsibility for all my sons when we got married. He always tried his best to be there for all my sons when they needed somebody.

Yossi and I now have two children. Our daughter's name is Tovah Leah; she lives in Tucson, Arizona and is continuing to pursue her degree. Our son Joshua lives in Florida and is going to school. Joshua made Aliyah right out of high school and lived in Israel for six years. He is an Israeli citizen and served in the IDF (Israel Defense Forces).

There are very few men like my husband, so determined to do his best in whatever comes his way. Yossi and I have been married now for 29 years. I can still depend on him to continue to pray for all our children. God is so faithful in keeping His promises. My whole family is in the hands of this Mighty God that I serve and love. I thank God for my husband. I have never met another man who remains so steady in all situations and makes the best of all circumstances. Most importantly, he remains a man steady and on course towards the will of God for our lives. I learned to live and raise my children in a Jewish home, practicing all the Biblical Jewish holidays and truly became a Ruth for these times. Truly I am living this verse:

> *Therefore, remember that formerly you who are Gentiles by birth and called "uncircumcised" by those who call themselves "the circumcision" (which is done in the body by human hands)— remember that at that time you were separate from Messiah, excluded from*

citizenship in Israel and foreigners to the covenants of the promise, without hope and without God in the world. But now in Messiah Yeshua you who once were far away have been brought near by the blood of Messiah. [Ephesians 2:11-13]

At the time of our marriage, there was so much hurt and disunity in the congregation, but the Lord used our marriage to bring unity and stability in the synagogue. The rabbi that married us remains our friend and brother in the Lord to this day. The congregation came together and we had such a huge reception that brought the Jew and Gentile to work together. It was an awesome wedding. Yossi and I had no other thought but to continue working for the Lord before and after our marriage.

A Voice of Wisdom

I have been in the Messianic movement now for 33 years. As I look back to earlier days in the movement, I realize it's no longer a movement. Messianic Synagogues are grounded and rooted to what they are supposed to be. There are numerous Messianic Synagogues in Israel now and more all over the world. The God of Abraham, Isaac and Jacob is working out the promised salvation spoken of in the Book of Romans.

> *I do not want you to be ignorant of this mystery, brothers and sisters, so that you may not be conceited: Israel has experienced a hardening in part until the full number of the Gentiles has come in, and in this way all Israel will be saved. As it is written:*
>
> *"The deliverer will come from Zion; He will turn godlessness away from Jacob. And this is My covenant with them when I take away their sins."* [Romans 11:25-27]

At the beginning of the movement, Messianic Jews were titled by most of the church, as being under the law. We were told there was no need for a synagogue and all Jews had to do was to convert to Christianity. A Baptist pastor told my husband there was no way he could be saved because there was no salvation left for the Jews. "You Jews had your chance," I remember him saying. This type of ignorance brings about anti-Semitism. It's the misunderstanding of prophetic Scripture. The Gentile Church needs to understand the times we are living in and the role God calls us as Gentiles to play.

At the time when Yeshua came to Israel, He fulfilled the prophecy of the Messiah coming to Israel. After the resurrection He instructed the disciples to take the Good News of salvation to the rest of the world. Which fulfilled the promise God made with Abraham that through his seed all nations would be blessed.

> *The Lord had said to Abram, "Go from your country, your people and your father's household to the land I will show you.*
>
> *"I will make you into a great nation, and I will bless you; I will make your name great, and you will be a blessing. I will bless those who bless you, and whoever curses you I will curse; and all peoples on earth will be blessed through you." [Genesis 12:1-3]*

After 33 years of being a Gentile in a Messianic synagogue, I still get the comment: "I don't know why you all think you have to have a synagogue instead of just joining the church." This is the way I understand Scripture. When Yeshua first came to Israel not all of Israel could have been saved. The plan of God for the salvation of the world had to initiate from Israel. Rav Shaul (Paul) was chosen to start this. The book of Romans tells us:

> *What then? What the people of Israel sought so earnestly they did not obtain. The elect among them did, but the others were hardened, as it is written:*
>
> *"God gave them a spirit of stupor, eyes that could not see and ears that could not hear, to this very day."*
>
> *And David says: "May their table become a snare and a trap, a stumbling block and a retribution for them. May their eyes be darkened so they cannot see, and their backs be bent forever."*

> *Again I ask: Did they stumble so as to fall beyond recovery? Not at all! Rather, because of their transgression, salvation has come to the Gentiles to make Israel envious.* [Romans 11:7-11]

God gave Israel a spirit of stupor, eyes they could not see, ears so they could not hear for the sake of the plan of God to bring salvation to the Gentile nations. The prophet Zechariah wrote:

> *This is what the Lord Almighty says: "In those days ten people from all languages and nations will take firm hold of one Jew by the hem of his robe and say, 'Let us go with you, because we have heard that God is with you.'"* [Zechariah 8:23]

If we don't recognize the times we are in, the Gentile Church will miss out on what God instructs it to do. Rav Shaul says it like this in Romans:

> *But if their transgression means riches for the world, and their loss means riches for the Gentiles, how much greater riches will their full inclusion bring!* [Romans 11:12]

Gentiles need to ask: How are we making Israel envious? Are we saying to the Jews they need to convert? Or are we showing them the cross and singing hymns like "Onward Christian Soldier" as they did during the burning of synagogues in times past? The Jews have gone through a lot of suffering to protect the word of God (Torah), and now it's time to love them into salvation through the precious blood of their and our Messiah.

> *I speak the truth in Messiah—I am not lying, my conscience confirms it through the Holy Spirit—I have great sorrow and unceasing anguish in my heart. For I could wish that I myself were cursed and cut off from Messiah for the sake of my people, those of my own race, the people of Israel. Theirs is the adoption to sonship; theirs the divine glory, the covenants, the receiving of the law, the temple worship and the promises. Theirs are the patriarchs, and from them*

is traced the human ancestry of the Messiah, Who is God over all, forever praised! Amen. [Romans 9:1-5]

Rav Shaul (Paul) loved the Jewish people and understood all they had to go through in order for God's plan of redemption to continue to the whole world. If there are questions concerning what we are to do for Israel and the Jewish people in our community, I want to suggest you read the book of Romans carefully and do what it tells you to do. It's time for the Gentile Church to get a better understanding of what is happening with Israel and the Jews, and adhere to the move of the Holy Spirit as He takes us back to be part of the commonwealth of Israel.

Consequently, you are no longer foreigners and strangers, but fellow citizens with God's people and also members of his household, built on the foundation of the apostles and prophets, with Messiah Yeshua Himself as the chief cornerstone. [Ephesians 2:19-20]

We are living in days where the evil one wants to interrupt God's plan concerning Israel and salvation of the Jewish people. There are teachings in the Church that there is no need for Messianic Judaism and that Jews have a covenant of salvation outside and separate of Yeshua. That is a lie that comes directly from the pit of hell. The Scripture tells us:

"Salvation is found in no one else, for there is no other Name under heaven given to mankind by which we must be saved." [Acts 4:12]

The whole world needs salvation through the atoning blood of our precious Yeshua. I don't understand how people justify what they dare to write.

For I am not ashamed of the gospel, because it is the power of God that brings salvation to everyone who believes: first to the Jew, then to the Gentile. For in the gospel the righteousness of God is revealed—a righteousness that is by faith from first to last, just as it is written: "The righteous will live by faith." [Romans 1:16-17]

As you see above, the Jew needs salvation as much as the Gentile. Yeshua's blood brings atonement for our sin. Jews remember this on Yom Kippur.

Our precious Jewish people need salvation (atonement) for their sins. God forbid I would consider not sharing the Good News of salvation to the Jewish community. Look at all the Jewish believers who live in Israel now. How can we justify this teaching? Some Churches say they stand with Israel, but do not stand with Messianic Jewish believers. Was it not because of Yeshua the Messiah that we get the term Messianic (Messiah)? We identify with Yeshua. The Jewish people are back and getting saved despite the erroneous teachings such as this one.

Another false teaching is the "Ephramite Error", also known as "Two House", that teaches all Gentiles who receive Yeshua are now physical Jews from the Tribe of Ephraim and that they now have the legitimate rights to the land of Israel. Not only does this rob the Jewish people of their identity and inheritance, but it also robs them of their God ordained ancestral land.

I am a Gentile and was called to identify with Israel. I have lived a Jewish lifestyle for 33 years, raised my children in a Jewish home, am the wife of a Messianic Rabbi, but I remain a Gentile by birth. To say all Gentiles are now Jewish is also a lie. There is a roll to play in God's plan for the redemption of the Jewish people. As Gentiles, we need to stand with Israel and the Jewish people as the times of restoring the Jewishness to the Gospel has arrived. The body of the Messiah needs to embrace Messianic Jews and support them. Israel and the Jewish people are getting saved. You have to make a decision to be a part of the work God is doing for these appointed times. Or you can say this does not concern me and continue as you are in regards to your thoughts about Messianic Judaism and the nation of Israel.

> *For I tell you that unless your righteousness surpasses that of the Pharisees and the teachers of the law, you will certainly not enter the kingdom of heaven.* [Matthew 5:20]

Why did the Pharisees and the teachers of the law miss the Messiah? Rav Shaul tells us in *Romans 11:7-8*, *"What then? What the people of Israel sought so earnestly they did not obtain. The elect among them did, but the others were hardened, as it is written: "God gave them a spirit of stupor, eyes that could not see and ears that could not hear, to this very day."*

Can you imagine if all of Israel had recognized Messiah? The message of salvation would not have come to the rest of the world as God promised Abraham. We read in *Genesis 12:2-3, "I will make you into a great nation, and I will bless you; I will make your name great, and you will be a blessing. I will bless those who bless you, and whoever curses you I will curse; and all peoples on earth will be blessed through you."*

First the Bible says God gave them a spirit of stupor (meaning a state of reduced sensibility; mental confusion; daze). I hear comments like, "I can't believe the Jews rejected Christ" or "The Jews have had their chance. Now they are condemned to hell." Obviously, those who were making such comments have never studied their Scriptures thoroughly. I believe with all my heart that God is speaking to the Gentile Churches to support the Messianic Jews as well as Israel as a nation. Scripture tell us:

It does not, therefore, depend on human desire or effort, but on God's mercy. [Romans 9 -11]

Moses was sent by the hand of the Lord to Pharaoh several times with divine instruction. However, God hardened Pharaoh's heart and he refused to obey the Word of the Lord. Likewise, God hardened the heart of the Jewish people in order to bring His plan of salvation to the Gentile nations. Why didn't the Pharisees and the Sadducees recognize Yeshua as the Messiah? Certainly, they knew the Scriptures and the words of the Prophets. Was it because they were too proud of their positions and place in the Synagogue? Had they become so religious, unwilling to change their minds, even in the midst of signs, wonders, and miracles? On several occasions, Yeshua pointed out their improper interpretation and understanding of the Scriptures. In the end, God hardened their hearts and opened the door for the Good News to go to a people that was not His own.

Could this happen to the Church today? Is the church so used of doing things a certain way. Why does most of the church close their eyes to Messianic Judaism as being a supernatural and a divine work of God? It is imperative that we remain a people of prayer and fasting, so that God does not have to harden our hearts and remove us from His sight. God's plan of salvation started with the Jewish people and will end with Yeshua coming back setting His feet on Mt. Zion.

> *If some of the branches have been broken off, and you, though a wild olive shoot, have been grafted in among the others and now share in the nourishing sap from the olive root, do not consider yourself to be superior to those other branches. If you do, consider this: You do not support the root, but the root supports you. You will say then, "Branches were broken off so that I could be grafted in." Granted. But they were broken off because of unbelief, and you stand by faith. Do not be arrogant, but tremble. 21 For if God did not spare the natural branches, he will not spare you either.* [Romans 11:17-21]

Since Messianic Jews have been in synagogues for so many years, I believe the Gentile Body of the Messiah needs to stop and re-think what Messianic Judaism is and how this will affect the body of the Messiah worldwide.

I have had the opportunity to sit and talk to a Rabbi of a Conservative Synagogue on several occasions. After meeting with him several times, I could see the Sprit of God drawing him to Yeshua. The one question he had was, "If Yeshua is the Jewish Messiah, why has He been turned into a Gentile?" The Jewish people are still looking for the Jewish Messiah, and therefore, we need to understand that the Jewish person does not need to convert to Christianity. They need to find atonement for their sin by recognizing their Jewish Messiah, Yeshua. The only converts in scripture were the Gentiles to Judaism. (In the book of Acts)

I was invited to a Passover Seder that was being held at the home of a couple who were Holocaust survivors. I let them know in advance that I attended a Messianic Jewish Synagogue. As we were talking, an older Jewish lady said to me, "I heard you are with the Jews for Jesus." I begin to explain to her about Messianic Judaism. The Jewish man who was hosting the Seder interrupted me and asked for my attention. He called his wife over and asked her to roll the sleeve on her blouse up and he did the same.

He then looked at me with such eyes of despair and said, pointing to the numbers on their arms, "this is what the name Jesus means to me."

What do you say to someone who lost all their family in the Holocaust? How do you introduce Yeshua to a Holocaust survivor? How do you comfort them? We all need to pray and ask the Lord how to reach His Jewish people.

I responded to him by saying how sorry I was they went through such horror. I told him that not everyone that calls themselves Christians live like Christians and therefore wind up miss-representing Yeshua. I went on to say to him, "If you would allow me, I would like to introduce Yeshua to you." A miracle took place there. All the sudden there was such a hush in the room, I knew God had shown up. The couple pulled a chair and sat down. He turned around and looked at me and said "Go ahead, I would like to hear what you have to say." I shared for about 20 minutes all that Yeshua said and did in Israel. Only God could have done that. There was such a presence of God in the room, I could almost see the finger of God reaching into their hearts to begin a healing that can only come from God Himself.

At the end of the Seder, the Jewish lady who asked me the question about the Jews for Jesus invited me to her apartment. She said she wanted to show me her furniture. We went to her apartment. My friend went with me. As we were walking around, I noticed she had an open Bible on her bed turned to *Isaiah 53*. "I see you read the Bible I said." She said "yes, but I don't understand it." Then she asked me if I could explain it to her. I spend a couple of hours at her apartment sharing scripture. At the end she asked me how she could accept Yeshua. She received her Messiah that day!

It was just like the account of Philip in Acts 8:26-31.

Now an angel of the Lord said to Philip, "Go south to the road—the desert road—that goes down from Jerusalem to Gaza." So he started out, and on his way he met an Ethiopian eunuch, an important official in charge of all the treasury of the Kandake (which means "queen of the Ethiopians"). This man had gone to Jerusalem to worship, and on his way home was sitting in his chariot reading the Book of Isaiah the prophet. The Spirit told Philip, "Go to that chariot and stay near it."

Then Philip ran up to the chariot and heard the man reading Isaiah the prophet. "Do you understand what you are reading?" Philip asked.

"How can I," he said, "unless someone explains it to me?" So he invited Philip to come up and sit with him.

These are just a couple of instances as to how the God of Abraham, Isaac and Jacob, through our precious Messiah Yeshua, are gathering the Jewish from all parts of the world.

If you do not support Messianic Judaism and the Jewish People, you need to pray because this is a divine move of God and you are coming against what God is doing in these last days to fulfill Scripture to see all Israel saved. We need to understand that Yeshua was the Jewish Messiah and His disciples were the original believers and the first Messianic Jews.

May God give us the grace, wisdom, knowledge and understanding to accomplish all that He calls us to do. Messiah is coming and will set foot on Mt. Zion. Let's get ready to meet the Lord. Let's finish the salvation calling: **"First to the Jew, then to the Gentile."**

EPILOGUE

When Yossi and I were planning our wedding, the Lord spoke to him about two Scriptures that would characterize our marriage. These Scriptures spoke vividly of how the unity between the Jew and Gentile would bring about many good works for the Kingdom of God. These words were inscribed on the cover of our wedding invitation.

> *For He himself is our peace, Who has made the two groups one and has destroyed the barrier, the dividing wall of hostility... For we are God's handiwork, created in Messiah Yeshua to do good works, which God prepared in advance for us to do.* [Ephesians 2:14 and 2:10]

In 1988, the rabbi of the Messianic Synagogue we were part of resigned due to family issues. As a result, Yossi and David Katz took over the leadership of the congregation for the next four years. In 1992 when David Katz and his family made Aliyah (immigration to Israel), Yossi became the full-time rabbi of the congregation for the next 12 years.

During this time we saw the Lord work in miraculous ways and numbers of Jewish people received Messiah Yeshua as their hope and redemption. And along with the promise to Abraham that all other nations would be blessed, we saw scores of Gentiles come to know the Jewish Messiah.

In 2004, in a miraculous manner, the Lord spoke to us and we moved to the west coast of Florida and attended Shoresh David Messianic Synagogue in Tampa. Within a few years the Lord spoke to Yossi and he took over as the rabbi of the Shoresh David Messianic Synagogue in Lakeland (now Etz Chayim Messianic Synagogue).

Through our 30 years of marriage, we have seen the above Scriptures come to life, and have been blessed to see hundreds of Jews and Gentiles receive Messiah Yeshua. However, I believe this is just the beginning and not the end. This is the beginning of a fountain opening up and the outpouring of redemption for the Jewish people which is the fulfillment in Zechariah where it says:

> *On that day a fountain will be opened to the house of David and the inhabitants of Jerusalem, to cleanse them from sin and impurity.* [Zechariah 13:1]

This is the fulfillment of Yom Kippur, a day of affliction, where upon Yeshua's return we will see our Jewish people finally recognize Yeshua as Messiah.

> *"And I will pour out on the house of David and the inhabitants of Jerusalem a spirit of grace and supplication. They will look on Me, the one they have pierced, and they will mourn for Him as one mourns for an only child, and grieve bitterly for Him as one grieves for a firstborn son."* [Zechariah 12:10]

Although we are older, and hopefully wiser, this is not the end of our story. It's just the beginning.